BALD HEAD ISLAND
The Early Years

Memories, Mishaps, and Merriment

Mary-Kathryn Moore
with Dalene Bickel

Copyright © 2022 by Moore Stories, LLC

All rights reserved. No part of this book may be reproduced in any form or by any means electronic or mechanical including but not limited to photocopying, recording, or any information storage and retrieval system, without the permission in writing from the author.

Although the publisher and the authors have made every effort to ensure that the information in this book was correct at the time of printing, and while this publication is designed to provide accurate information in regard to the subject matter covered, the publisher and the authors assume no responsibility for errors, inaccuracies, omissions, or any other inconsistencies herein and hereby disclaim any liability to any party for any loss, damage, or disruption caused by errors or omissions, whether such errors or omissions result from negligence, accident, or any other cause.

Cover and interior design by Michael C. Cadieux

Cover photo by Patrick McGowan

ISBN 9780578363738

Contents

Introduction 4

The Vision
Carolina Cape Fear Corporation
Chapter 1 – Development Plan Highlights 9
Chapter 2 – Selling the Concept 13

Pioneer Years (1970s)
The First Families
Chapter 3 – The Generator Society 18
Chapter 4 – Music to the Ears 20

Access Adventures
Chapter 5 – River Crossings 24
Chapter 6 – Driving on Sand 29
Chapter 7 – Runway Landings 34

The First Homes
Chapter 8 – Named by Necessity 41
Chapter 9 – The Old Boat House 42
Chapter 10 – Skylark 44
Chapter 11 – Raccoon Hilton 46
Chapter 12 – Happy House 48
Chapter 13 – MilBo Hilton 50
Chapter 14 – Rockhound 52
Chapter 15 – Pilot House 53
Chapter 16 – The Seven C's 55
Chapter 17 – Neptune 56
Chapter 18 – The Sandfiddler 58
Chapter 19 – C Turtle 60
Chapter 20 – Captain Charlie's Station 61
Chapter 21 – Tree House 63
Chapter 22 – Blue Crab 67
Chapter 23 – Hickory Nut 68
Chapter 24 – Sand Dollar 69
Chapter 25 – Young One 70
Chapter 26 – Hilltop 72
Chapter 27 – Cunningham House 73

The Expansion

Chapter 28 – Bald Head Island Property Owners Association .... 75 (BHI POA)
Chapter 29 – BHI Limited 80
Chapter 30 – Bald Head Association & the Village 87

Outfitter Years (1980s)

The Big Event
Chapter 31 – Power to the People. 91
Landmark Structures
Chapter 32 – Bald Head Inn. 97
Chapter 33 – Old Baldy Lighthouse 105
Chapter 34 – Village Chapel 106
Outfitter Experiences
Chapter 35 – Official Outfitters 115
Chapter 36 – Sanctuary. 120
Chapter 37 – The Hobbit Hole 121
Chapter 38 – Pure Madness … and Magic. 122
Chapter 39 – Poncho & Fainting Joe Hill. 124
Chapter 40 – Legends, Nobles & Scalawags 126
Chapter 41 – The Car Bar. 128
Chapter 42 – The Bench Without an Arm 129
Chapter 43 – You'll Get a Lot of Reading Done 130
Chapter 44 – A Golf Cart that Died … and a Dog that Didn't . . . 131
Chapter 45 – On the Fine Art of Gillnetting 133

The Legacy

Nature & Conservancy
Chapter 46 – The Lure of the Landscape 141
Chapter 47 – Critters for Company 144
Chapter 48 – The Conservancy. 154
Community & Camaraderie
Chapter 49 – Leisurely Lifestyle 161
Chapter 50 – Surviving the Storms. 170
Chapter 51 – That's Just the Way It Was. 173

Acknowledgments 178

About the Author 179

Introduction

In December 2020, nine months into the COVID-19 pandemic, the idea for this book was born. For seven months, my husband, daughter, and I lived on Bald Head Island in the same condo that I have been coming to my entire life, the one that my grandparents, Carol and Draden Moore, bought in 1983.

Living on the island caused me to reflect, not for the first time, about my summers growing up there: My first kiss, being swept out to sea in a rip current, my dad picking me up and away from an alligator while fishing. Listening to the CB radio, my brother's little green bike, climbing the steps to the top of Old Baldy. Watching baby foxes run in the forest, dolphins swimming beside my kayak in the marsh, crabbing and clamming with my family. Turtles laying eggs under the starry nights. The jumping mullet show and the eels in the lagoons. Swimming out to the sandbars at Frying Pan Shoals, a raccoon chasing me and then my dad chasing the raccoon.

I feel closer to the natural world on BHI than anywhere else. It draws me in, constantly reminding me it's where I'm most content: together with nature, wild and free.

Even today, as I ride the ferry and watch BHI come into view, I eagerly anticipate entering a place set apart from the rest of the world, one that offers a dreamlike existence. The island becomes my fairytale abode—a private kingdom that holds my father's and grandparents' spirits.

Bald Head Island is breathtakingly beautiful and offers a simple life that runs on turtle time. It's one of a kind, and attracts its own kind. It was these people that my grandparents introduced me to as a child—the island property owners of the 1970s and 1980s who created a thriving community without modern conveniences.

It was the Wild West back then and preserving those types of crazy stories was why I decided to write this book. From the start I knew I wanted to create not only a keepsake for islanders, but also a historical, regional-interest book that would appeal to a wider audience as well. And it had to be fun—an adventure in itself to read!

Once the idea took hold of me, there was no turning back. It consumed me for all of 2021 and I am so happy that it did. I had an amazing time connecting with so many of BHI's early population and their family members. I spent most of my daughter's nap times reading through the Old Baldy Foundation's online archives, thrilled at the discovery of each new detail and story.

Over the last year, as the stories became chapters and the book began to take shape, it reminded me of the slow growth and cohesiveness of the early years on Bald Head Island. It is my hope that this book showcases the camaraderie and ingenuity of the Generator Society that still influences the culture of BHI today.

For me, Bald Head Island will forever be my happy place. I hope that this book allows you, too, in some small way, to appreciate the splendor and the distinction of the island and its people.

—*Mary-Kathryn Moore*

To James Draden Moore V (Papa), Carol Saulsbury Moore (Nana), and James Draden "Jay" Moore VI (Dad) for instilling the love of Bald Head Island in me and providing Emma Jay the same opportunity to experience it as well. I'm eternally grateful.

PART I: THE VISION

"A special place for special people."
—A Concept Study for the Development of Bald Head Island North Carolina

Carolina Cape Fear Corporation

Chapter 1
Development Plan Highlights

Bald Head Island (BHI) has a long and storied past. Originally referred to as Cape Island, it and the neighboring Middle and Bluff Islands were purchased by Landgrave Thomas Smith in 1713 and renamed Smith Island Complex. For more than 250 years the name stuck. In fact, some locals still refer to it as Smith Island and a current conservancy group is named SILT (Smith Island Land Trust). Throughout much of that time, the 12,000-acre island harbored only wildlife, pirates, and the occasional soldier. During the Civil War, for example, the confederates temporarily moved in and constructed Fort Holmes.

During the nineteenth and early twentieth centuries, the U.S. Government took an interest in the island, constructing Old Baldy Lighthouse, the Cape Fear Life Saving Station, Federal Road, Cape Fear Lighthouse (including Captain Charlie's Station), and the U.S. Coast Guard Station.

But still, by late 1969, most people had little knowledge of or interest in what had by then become known as Bald Head Island. Rumor has it that the name derived from the tall mounded dunes that, when seen at a distance by plane or ship, resembled a man's bald head.

Once the nine founders of Carolina Cape Fear Corporation (CCFC) learned of the island, however, they saw potential. When they met for their first brainstorming session in January 1970, they envisioned an exclusive residential community that would simultaneously protect and preserve the island's natural landscape, causing Bald Head Island to become known as a top destination for outdoor recreation.

Rainbow connecting Bluff and Middle Islands. Bluff Island is on the right; Middle Island is on the left. The middle part of the photo is the marsh between the two islands. Photo courtesy of Pat and Charlie Young.

The need for such a community was supported by an *Architectural Record* editorial dated May 1970, in which some experts predicted that, by the year 2000, there would be an "increase of 141 percent in outdoor recreation, and a 60 percent increase between 1965 and 1980." Thus, CCFC desired to develop the island at "a high level of design" in order to "provide for the leisure time needs for people of many tastes"[1] for the foreseeable future.

To help them in their marketing efforts, they enlisted the architectural and engineering firm Wm. F. Freeman Associates to create a "Concept Study for the Development of Bald Head Island North Carolina." The plan outlined six proposed growth stages with estimated completion dates. As with most large-scale developments, however, the plan met with paperwork snafus, regulatory delays, public outcries, and underestimated expenses, leading Carolina Cape Fear Corporation to make several revisions over the years and to scrap certain ideas altogether.

Today's residents and visitors, for example, aren't able to rent a horse from a stable, admire a panoramic view from atop a Ferris wheel, or purchase luxury brands from an upscale shopping center. They are, however, able to choose from a variety of recreational activities intended to connect visitors with the natural landscape, such as meandering through the maritime forest, kayaking along the creek, playing a round of golf on BHI's signature course, or enjoying a bonfire on the beach with family and friends.

In the end, CCFC and its successors managed to successfully balance development with preservation.

---

[1] "A Concept Study for the Development of Bald Head Island North Carolina" by Wm. F. Freeman Associates.

Overview of the original 1970 development plan:

Stage I (to begin October 1970)
500-room hotel
420-room motel
210-unit apartments
500-unit condominium
1,320 single-family lots
Ferry slip & dock
Lighthouse village
Country club & golf course

Stage II (to begin July 1975)
Tennis & beach clubs
Stage III (to begin January 1979)
Marsh cottage on creek-front lot
Stage IV (to begin July 1981)
Yacht club

Stage V (to begin January 1984)
Marina Village
Condominiums
Stables

Stage VI (to begin July 1986)
620-unit motel
310-unit apartments
Shopping center
Amusement park
Boardwalk & public beach
Utility Area & right of way
Beach & inlet protection

Images on pages 10-11 are from the development plan, "A Concept Study for the Development of Bald Head Island North Carolina" by Wm. F. Freeman Associates.

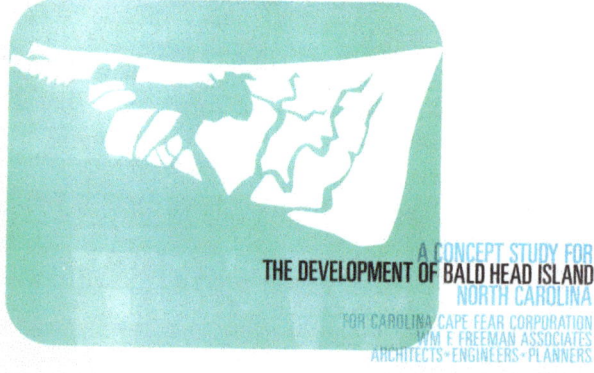

Proposed plan of Carolina Cape Fear Corporation. 1972. Photo courtesy of Harriet and Cindy Poole.

Chapter 2
Selling the Concept

From the outset, Carolina Cape Fear Corporation understood that Bald Head Island was "a special place for special people"[2] and recognized that, in order to turn their vision into reality, they needed to locate successful businessmen and their families who possessed not only the requisite investment funds, but also the physical stamina and intrepid personalities necessary to endure the challenges of constructing homes in relative isolation.

They kick-started their search in the spring of 1970 by sending press releases, mailing letters, and giving presentations throughout North Carolina. Bill Henderson, CEO and President of CCFC, personally met with doctors, attorneys, politicians, business owners, and corporate executives in corporate board rooms and private residences—one-on-one and in small groups.

Watts and Betsy Carr attended one of those first meetings when Henderson's team traveled to their hometown of Durham. "We loved the plans for a low-key, environmentally sensitive, premier development," Watts says, "and we, together with Betsy's sister Genevieve Cummings and her husband, Tom, bought into the action with a CCFC package of stock and an ocean front lot."

Several other families elected to purchase stock as well, which obliged them to buy one lot initially and a second lot at a later date. Estate packages were also offered, which included two lots and one membership to the Bald Head Island Golf and Country Club, or families could purchase the basic two-lot package deal (which offered a 10 percent discount on the second lot). The limit of two lots, selected by lottery and rarely adjoining each other, ensured the construction of single-resident homes rather than commercial structures.

The referrals of these early buyers became CCFC's main marketing arm. Since there were a finite number of lots available in the proposed low-density community, the property owners wanted their close friends and colleagues to share in the opportunity before it was too late, especially once CCFC began to expand its marketing efforts beyond the state of North Carolina in 1974. Cindy Poole remembers hearing northern accents at the pool after they started advertising in the *Wall Street Journal*.

Interestingly, the Carrs were already familiar with Bald Head Island. The couple had first learned about BHI in 1968 from their local paper, the *News and Observer*, when it ran an article about how Charles Fraser of Hilton Head was attempting to acquire and develop the island in the same environmentally sound manner he had successfully done with Sea Pines Plantation in South Carolina. The couple's first visit to BHI was in 1969 when twenty-six-year-old Watts met with Fraser in the hopes of working with him.

---

[2] Inscription inside "A Concept Study for the Development of Bald Head Island North Carolina" given to Earl and Kitty Congdon, June 7, 1976.

However, Fraser soon tired of fighting bureaucratic red tape and gave up on the project, causing Watts to look elsewhere for a job. Nevertheless, BHI was destined to be a part of their lives. "We rented there over the years before we finally built our own home in 1982," he says.

As CCFC continued to promote residential opportunities for families on Bald Head Island, it also moved forward with its own commercial development projects. By 1972 they were still in the process of clearing land for an eighteen-hole golf course but had completed the Bald Head Inn. Prospective property owners were invited to visit the island, stay at the inn, and fall in love with the beauty and potential of the island.

Bill and Billie Jean Berne were one of four couples from Lumberton who decided to take the developers up on the offer to visit. In March 1972, the Bernes, Westers, Millers, and Wards drove to Southport where they were ushered aboard small boats and transported across the Cape Fear River to the island.

"It was miserable weather," Billie Jean recalls. "Alternately, it rained, sleeted, and snowed. The lots were not cleared, the roads were dirt, and there was a lot of construction going on for the golf course. It was a mess."

Nevertheless, each of the four families bought a two-lot package deal that day. They joked that the agent went home and said, "Honey, if I can sell four lots on a horrible day like today, then I can sell anything!"

The Westers and the Bernes immediately began constructing their island homes and quickly became part-time residents. The Millers and Wards later sold their lots.

Gene and Joyce Douglas bought the Millers' golf course lot in 1973. "My whole family fell in love with Bald Head Island," Gene recalls. "We vacationed there annually and stayed at the inn; my four children never wanted to go anywhere else." The couple eventually retired to BHI in 1995, becoming year-round residents.

It should be noted that not everyone learned about the island through CCFC's carefully planned marketing efforts. John and Sheila May, for example, became interested after hearing offhand rumors and a piece of negative press. "Carolina Cape Fear Corporation's office was on Howe Street in Southport, in the vicinity of a church and a liquor store, giving rise to stories about how they had all their bases covered," Sheila explains. "We had also read about a controversy between the developer and preservation groups who wanted to keep the island undeveloped by having the state buy it. These articles made the island sound so attractive that we decided to visit in 1973. The real estate agent took us fishing and when we promptly caught a nice puppy drum, we were hooked and bought property that day."

Over the next decade, additional investors bought island property, but only a handful of families joined the Westers and Bernes as homeowners and part-time residents. This latter group quickly banded together, giving themselves the moniker "The Generator Society" —a nod to their reliance on propane, gasoline, and diesel generators to fuel their island life.

The official patch of the Generator Society members, circa 1980.

PART II: PIONEER YEARS (1970s)

"The Generator Society was a close-knit group of people who were very well off in the business world but enjoyed semi-roughing it on an island."
—James Poole

The First Families

Chapter 3
The Generator Society

1972[3]
Buck and Becky Bunn
- Davis
- Lee
- Bunny
- Nancy

1973
Bill and Billie Jean Berne
- Dabney
- David
- Jeff

Thad and Lee Wester
- Ellen
- Bryan
- Ginny
- Amanda

1974
Pat and Jo Thomas
- Patsy
- Andy
- Leslie

Bo and Mildred Caperton
- Millie
- Amelia

Joe and Buris Crowell
- Joe Crowell, Jr.

Jimmy and Margaret Harper

1975
Ken and Eleanor Cosgrove
- Kenneth
- Timothy
- Barry
- Jeff
- Christopher

Bynum Tudor

1976
Charlie and Patricia Young
- Delice
- Fred
- Glenda
- David
- Kevin
- Sheila

Billy and Charlotte Dunlap
- Marshall
- Wick

---
[3] Years represent occupancy dates, not purchase dates.

1977

Earl and Kitty Congdon
- Audrey
- Karen
- David

Robin and Barbara Hayes
- Winslow
- Bob

Frank and Harriet Poole
- Jim
- Bill
- Cindy

1978

Cash and Irma Caroon
- Donald
- Lionel
- Keith
- Adam

Bill and Pat Cunningham
- Chip

1979

Harry and Elva Schmulling
- Henry
- Carolyn
- Elva
- Catherine

Reddy and Bippie Grubbs
- Mike
- Steve
- Nan

Chapter 4
Music to the Ears

For Bald Head Island property owners accustomed to conveniences such as refrigerators, washing machines, electric lights, and central heat, the sudden lack of them—as well as of running water—was more than an inconvenience. It was a serious problem that required an immediate solution.

Enter the generator.

This small piece of machinery enabled the pioneers to power their water pumps and prized appliances … a few at a time. Every homeowner purchased at least one generator (some bought two) to meet their family's overwhelming desire to flush a toilet, take a shower, and see at night. Human habits, after all, are hard to break. "It's funny how you automatically flip switches and push buttons, power or no," Pat Cunningham recalls. "We were constantly amused at our dependence on electricity."

The generator brands and power capacities varied according to the needs and personalities of each homeowner—just like the houses they built. The Congdons, for example, used their generator as little as possible and never for lights, opting instead to use kerosene lamps. The Cunninghams used theirs only at night and the Hayes limited usage to the lights and water pump. The Westers connected kitchen appliances and a heating/cooling system to their generator, but never all at once, whereas the Capertons ran almost all of their electricity at one time. The Caroons started up their generator as often as needed, day or night.

And while they were thankful for this apparatus that enabled them to sporadically enjoy their creature comforts, they quickly discovered that every generator had two major flaws.

The first became apparent as soon as a generator roared to life. Without any volume control, its distinctive rumble and whir drowned out any other sound around it. Buck Bunn and his family refrained from using their generator at night precisely because "it made such a racket," and Jeff Cosgrove recalls his father building a shed in an effort to reduce the noise. The generators were so loud that they seemed to go against the developer's commitment to protecting the island's visible—and audible—beauty. As the original plan stated, "in order to enhance the character of natural beauty, the sounds of nature must be heard."

"The quietness of the island—absolute silence—was a treasure enjoyed by all," admits Bill Berne. "But the generator noise was music to the ears when one needed what it provided."

And, one might add, it was music to the ears when it worked. It quickly became apparent that generators were not only noisy, but they were unreliable as well.

It mattered not whether they were one kilowatt or sixty-five kilowatt, old or new; they seemed to have minds of their own. Thad Wester valiantly scheduled generator checks every three weeks, but even he frequently dealt with an ornery piece of equipment. Millie Caperton McVey remembers using lots of candlelight as the generator was "not dependable" and Eleanor Cosgrove vividly recalls what became a regular occurrence: "There's nothing like driving seven hours to Southport, enduring a bumpy boat ride, and arriving with a houseful of guests and family only to discover an uncooperative generator."

Such unreliability, as well as the rising cost of diesel fuel, prompted several families to install gas appliances such as stoves, refrigerators, and water heaters. It also led Bobby McMahon to build a 210-gallon water tank in the attic. A generator pumped water up into the tank until it was filled, and gravity ensured a reliable water source. The ingenuity of this idea caught on. Soon, others installed tanks of their own to replace the outdoor hand pumps that tended to rust to the point of being unusable—forcing homeowners to draw water in pails from nearby lagoons with which to cook, brush, and flush.

The longer the residents stayed, the more innovative they became. In order to operate additional electronic devices, Billy Dunlap and his brother-in-law Bobby McMahan designed a car battery that could be connected to two small generators that they used to power vacuum cleaners, hair dryers, a tape deck, and even a small black-and-white television set—which received up to three stations if they adjusted the rabbit ears (antenna) just right. Frank Poole solved the universal bedtime challenge of turning off the generator and then trying to trek to the bedroom in the dark without stubbing a toe. According to his wife, Harriet, "He designed an ingenious bedside turn-off switch for the generator that ran the lights, small appliances, and luxuries such as the television and electric blankets."

Yet despite the noise and unreliability of the generators, no one could deny their importance. Therefore, most of the homeowners built sheds to protect their generators from the relentless and damaging salt air, sometimes doing so with flair. Thad Wester, for example, altered a Western Electric sign so that it read "Wester Electric" and hung it on an outside wall for all to see.

As the Generator Society membership certificate summarizes: "During the early years of development and modernization of Bald Head Island, there were families who endured inconvenience and privation in exchange for the privilege of being married to Bald Head in a unique way known only to a few."[4]

---

[4] Old Baldy Foundation Subject Files, "Generator Society Members List," accessed February 15, 2022, https://drive.google.com/drive/folders/1Q8lYoRCwk5dWBszqxBOpqtqOAUQM57oM.

The First Families and Their Generators

Bunn	Sears 1 kW
Berne	Onan 45 kW diesel
Wester	Onan 3 kW gas and Onan 6 kW diesel
Thomas	Kirloskar 7 kW and Onan 17.5 kW
Caperton	(Brand unknown) 17 kW diesel
Crowell	(Brand unknown) 25 kW gas
Harper	Onan 5 kW
Cosgrove	(Brand and size unknown, although one of the boys remembers it as an "old, cheap-o Army generator" that he coined a "Rube Goldberg"—a contraption that "performs a very basic job in a complicated way.")[5]
Young	Onan 2 kW diesel
Dunlap	Briggs and Stratton 3 kW gas
Congdon	Onan 17 kW
Hayes	Homelite 5 kW
Poole	Honda 1.5 kW
Caroon	Onan 5 kW diesel
Cunningham	Onan 5 kW
Schmulling	Onan 65 kW diesel
Grubbs	Indian 9 kW diesel
Tudor	Onan 17 kW diesel

---

[5] National Center for Families Learning, "What Is a Rube Goldberg Machine?" accessed February 10, 2022, https://www.wonderopolis.org/wonder/what-is-a-rube-goldberg-machine.

Access Adventures

Chapter 5
River Crossings

Over the years, the merits of a bridge connecting Bald Head Island to the mainland have been debated, but the allure of the island continues to rest in its remoteness and sparse population—undeniably aided by its limited access. While the current ferry system runs like clockwork, and fully functioning marinas along the Cape Fear River offer private boat owners direct access,[6] this was not the case for the early pioneers. Not only did they have to schedule their passage with the developer's boatmen well in advance, but they also had to time their arrivals and departures with the tides in order to successfully land at Bald Head Creek.

Penn Yan boat heading towards Southport from the Bald Head Creek access. Photo courtesy of Harriet and Cindy Poole.

Depending on the size of the traveling party, one or more of these captains would be waiting at the Southport dock to load their clients' luggage and transport them across the swift and dangerous Cape Fear River before navigating up Bald Head Creek. Locating the small floating dock was sometimes a challenge, especially at night when the thin flickering beam of a flashlight barely extended beyond the bow of the boat.

---

[6] Bald Head Island's first passenger ferry, *Bald Head I*, launched in 1976. According to James Poole, "It was really a treat," but since the ferry's schedule proved to be erratic, some of the property owners continued to use their own boats.

As one can imagine, such trips didn't always go smoothly. One time, Vicki Young and a group of family and friends headed to BHI in two boats—one containing the men and the other containing Vicki, her ten-week-old son, a babysitter who couldn't swim, and a friend who was six-months pregnant. As they moved up the creek with the dock in sight, Vicki and her fellow passengers were suddenly jolted in their seats when their boat hit a sandbar. "They wanted us to try to walk the rest of the way in," she recalls, "but there were deep holes around and we refused. After about an hour of work in the hot August sun, they were able to get us free."

Returning to the mainland didn't guarantee smooth sailing or landing, either. Before Deep Point Marina and Indigo Plantation Marina were built, the downtown dock in Southport was the only access point. Yet sometimes it proved unsafe for larger boats to use, particularly during bad weather. Mrs. Dale Georgaide recalls one particular landing when strong winds and rough water caused a few anxious moments. Since their boat was unable to dock, the adults were instructed to climb down into a smaller boat that had been brought out to them. Once they were safely aboard, a crew member from the larger vessel tossed their children over the side to them.

Moore Street dock looking toward Bald Head Island. Courtesy of Nancy Giacci.

Moore Street dock 1987

Moore Street dock facing Southport. Courtesy of Nancy Giacci.

Unsurprisingly, many of the pioneers opted to purchase and use their own boats when possible. The Dunlaps, for example, obtained a nineteen-foot Renken, and the Crowells purchased a twenty-two-foot McKee Craft, which they used to transport whatever supplies, furniture, and appliances would fit.

This, of course, led to additional mishaps and adventures. One time the Congdons shuttled their guests across the river in the early morning but didn't make it back to the island before low tide. They were forced to abandon their nineteen-foot Whaler and wade to shore. When they returned later to retrieve the boat, they were surprised to discover that someone had already pulled it up onto dry ground for them.

Tides weren't the only challenges with which boat owners contended; fog often proved to be a frightening foe as well. One evening Joe Crowell Jr. and a friend were out on the open water when fog quickly rolled in, disorienting them. Hearing foghorns, they followed the sound, thinking they were being led safely back to dry land. Instead, they almost ran into a Coast Guard ship well out to sea. Patricia Young also recalls one river crossing that was so foggy a shrimp boat had to assist them with its radar. And fog almost ruined Martha Bumgarner's honeymoon.

Martha and her new husband, Merle, looked forward to a relaxing honeymoon on Bald Head Island. With a pan of lasagna her mother had made for them, a bottle of wine, and some luggage, the couple boarded a small Penn Yan (similar to a Jon boat) for the river crossing. Martha remembers how they slowly maneuvered through choppy water and thick fog. "All of a sudden, there was a freight ship right in front of us. I mean, it looked like the *Titanic*. Spunky, the captain, looked very nervous and his eyes grew bigger than his wire-rimmed glasses."

The ship blew its horn but they couldn't turn back because the wake from the cargo ship was so large it would have toppled their small boat. "So Spunky gunned it," Martha says. "I went from worrying about losing the lasagna to thinking I'm going to lose my life. I just wanted to drink a little wine and eat my mom's homemade lasagna on my honeymoon … Merle had never even been in a boat on the open waters before. What a start!"

Billy Dunlap, his brother-in-law Bobby McMahon, and two other men also dealt with a thick blanket of fog one morning as they headed out by motorboat to pick up a new wood stove. Despite their neglect to bring along a compass or radio, the men felt confident they could safely navigate to Oak Island and back since they were familiar with the route. However, long after their watches told them they should have arrived, there was still no land in sight. Forced to admit they were lost, they decided to continue heading straight. As they strained their eyes in the thick gray mist, they eventually spotted a buoy that indicated they had gone almost a quarter of a mile south into the open ocean rather than west along the coast. They turned the boat around and managed to land safely back at BHI before their fuel ran out.

As if ferrying people and small luggage to the island wasn't enough of a challenge, the Generator Society also faced significant difficulties getting construction materials delivered to their new homesites despite the provision by the CCFC developers of a barge and a war-surplus LST (Landing Ship Tank).

"At the time there was no barge landing, so sometimes the captains couldn't get the vessel all the way up on West Beach, depending on the tide," Billie Jean Berne explains. On one occasion her husband, Bill, had borrowed a plumber's work truck to haul small supplies from Lumberton to the island. When it was time to return the truck, Bill asked the captain of the barge to bring it closer so he could drive the truck onto it. Despite the tide coming in, the captain couldn't get it any closer. When Bill voiced his concern over the amount of water separating the truck from the barge, the captain replied, "That's as close as I can get and you better hurry up because it's getting worse." Bill reportedly shut his eyes a moment before gunning the truck over the dune and driving through the water onto the barge.

Bald Head I. Photo courtesy of Carol and Draden Moore.

Joe Crowell remembers that the early barge couldn't haul large construction trucks. This meant that all building supplies had to be handled four times: "They were put on a truck in Southport, loaded by hand onto the barge (often while wading through water), unloaded by hand onto a four-wheel-drive vehicle waiting on the island, and unloaded again at the homesite."

Bill Cunningham gives Mr. Joyner, his contractor, credit for perseverance. "Building on Bald Head Island got so complicated that one time, when the developer's lease for the barge expired, we arranged for a shrimp boat to bring building materials over for us." Additionally, Mr. Joyner faced staffing shortages. "Some of his workers quit because they were afraid of that trip across the river."

The swift-flowing mouth of the Cape Fear River has long been known for its strength and volatility as it enters the Atlantic Ocean at the southern tip of Bald Head Island. Pat Cunningham recalls how the river claimed their washing machine when it fell off the truck as it was being loaded onto the barge. Then, shortly thereafter, choppy water threatened to launch all their furnishings off the barge.

"It was all part of the island adventure," Joe Crowell explains matter-of-factly.

Bald Head I. Courtesy of Melinda Freeman.

Chapter 6
Driving on Sand

Today, Bald Head Island is replete with paved roads, sidewalks, and large wooden boardwalks. Yet aside from a few maintenance or construction vehicles, automobiles are notably absent. The only modes of transportation you see are electric golf carts and bicycles as they smoothly—and silently—glide along pathways.

It hasn't always been that way. In the 1970s, the Generator Society quickly discovered that golf carts are easily mired in sandy roads—the only kind of roads available at that time. Thus, in order to effectively explore the island and transport their belongings from the dock to their homes, each family relied on their own four-wheel drive.

South Bald Head Wynd with a few houses in the background. Courtesy of Harriet and Cindy Poole.

It wasn't long before everyone could identify who was coming down the lane based on the make and model of the vehicle. The Bunns, for example, sported the only 1964 Volkswagen Beetle on the island. The Thomas family opted for a dune buggy—a fun and smart choice for beach driving. The Schmullings owned a truck that generally served them well, but Elva's temptation to "splash and dash" was too great on at least one occasion, causing all four of her truck's wheels to sink into the sand while the tide was coming in.

The Pooles started with a dune buggy during their camping days, traded up to a station wagon during the construction days, and finished with a 1946 Jeep (which hauled a trailer outfitted with a bench and canopy for group travel).

Harriet and Frank Poole in their dune buggy with unknown man on the beach.

Frank Poole driving his Jeep with additional seating.
Courtesy of Harriet and Cindy Poole.

The Poole's well-used Jeep.
Photo courtesy of Harriet and Cindy Poole.

The Cosgroves started out with a Chevy Blazer and later exchanged it for an old mail Jeep, which took them right out onto the Point. In fact, one of the Cosgrove boys (who will remain anonymous) used the Jeep to take a friend fishing there one night. After the young men situated their poles out the windows of the vehicle, they had a few beers and got comfortable. In the pitch-dark stillness of the night, sleep soon overtook them until the sound of water splashing against the sides of the Jeep awoke them. Suddenly alert, they jumped into the water and ran to Charlie Young's house for assistance; fortunately, he was able to tow their Jeep from the surf before it was fully submerged.

The Capertons, Dunlaps, and Grubbs also owned Jeeps. Bo and Mildred Caperton's granddaughter, Millie Caperton McVey, remembers riding on the tailgate of her grandparents' blue Jeep, which they dubbed the "BoMobile." Bo always asked the grandchildren if they were safely seated and ready to go, not moving until he heard them respond, "Contact!" They would then take off along the sand roads to East Beach where they would look for conch shells.

Jeff Jorgensen (left, grandson of Bo and Mildred Caperton) and friend in 1977. Notice the tall antenna for their CB radio. This International Harvester Scout was the Caperton's vehicle before the blue "BoMobile" Jeep. Photo courtesy of Jeff Jorgensen.

Charlotte Dunlap also took family and friends to East Beach ... but experienced a couple of unplanned walks home. After one morning at the beach, she and a friend—and five eight-year-old girls—discovered the Jeep stuck in sand. They were forced to trek home, stopping at the Congdons to report the stranded vehicle along the way. Another time, Charlotte, a friend, and twelve preteens enjoyed a late-afternoon hot dog cookout on the beach before discovering the Jeep again mired in sand, this time below the tide line. With no other options, they walked down Federal Road. "Federal Road in the dark was quite scary back in the days when hardly anyone was on the island," Charlotte explains. "My friend led us in song to keep our minds off the ever-darkening sky and we made it back without being attacked by the Bald Head spirits purportedly lurking in the woods."

Memories equally abound for Billie Jean Berne regarding their International Harvester Scout. Shortly after the completion of their house, they invited two couples to spend a week with them at BHI. Upon arrival the ladies took the kids to the beach while the men stayed behind to hook up the CB radio. "I had never driven a car on the beach before but I thought, 'What can be so hard about that? Bill does it all the time,'" Billie Jean recalls. Mustering confidence, she drove the Scout onto South Beach where they all unloaded and explored. When Billie Jean realized that the boys were out of sight, she and her companions decided to get in the vehicle and drive around to find them.

They didn't go very far.

"I promptly stuck the car in sand up to the axle and the tide was coming in quickly." Knowing they needed assistance, she sent one friend to walk the beach to look for the boys, instructed the other friend to stay put, and began the walk back to her house on Fort Holmes Trail, stopping by the Wester's house along the way. "I went flying into their house yelling, 'I've lost the children! They're probably in the water and I'm never going to see them again!'"

Federal Road. Original artwork by Patricia Young.

Thad offered to drive down and look for them while Billie Jean ran the rest of the way to her house, where she found Bill and their guests having drinks. After assuring her that the boys were probably okay, Bill tried out the new CB. Thad responded that he found the boys walking down Federal Road unharmed. Billie Jean insisted that Thad put them on the radio. "I asked them, 'Why did you do that? Why didn't you come back?' And my oldest, Dabney, said, 'But Mommy, we found you some pretty shells.'"

Perhaps because of this incident, Bill and Billie Jean decided to periodically test their boys' navigational skills by dropping them off at various locations around the island at night to see if they could find their way back to the house. "They usually beat us back because they would cut through the woods or across the golf course while we had to drive along the roads, but sometimes it would take them some time."

All three of the Berne boys learned to drive on the island and did so at a much younger age than their friends on the mainland did. "Amanda Wester and Dabney worked at the inn when they were twelve and thirteen as a dishwasher and a waitress," Billie Jean recalls. "They used to take turns driving to and from work. David got a job driving golf carts from the storage shed to the golf shop and back at the end of the day."

The Congdons and Cunninghams also drove an International Harvester Scout, as did Gene Douglas. Gene remembers driving his Scout at full moon from the Point (where South Beach and East Beach converge) to Frying Pan Shoals without coming near the water.

Regardless of what type of vehicle the Generator Society members owned, getting stuck on the beach was a regular occurrence. Yet, without fail, each vehicle was pulled safely beyond the reach of the rising tides by neighbors who willingly dropped whatever they were doing to offer assistance.

"Those days were really something special," Bill Cunningham concedes. "I'm glad we knew Bald Head Island then."

Rainbow over South Beach. Photo courtesy of Melinda Freeman.

Chapter 7
Runway Landings

In 1977, another group made an appearance on the island: Bald Head Aviators. These fearless adventurers, less than half of them members of the Generator Society, provided the funding for a private airstrip along South Beach.

Pat Thomas, a pilot who owned a tail-dragger Cessna 310, spearheaded the project. According to his daughter Leslie, "My dad was a bit of an adrenaline junkie, a true daredevil—fishing, scuba diving, etc. He got his pilot's license at a young age but put it on the back burner for a long time, until we kids were growing up."

Leslie remembers when construction equipment dragged the road in front of the Thomas house, leveling it into the landing strip. According to an official Bald Head Aviator document dated Labor Day, September 5, 1977,[7] the 2300 x 75-foot airstrip would be graded, irrigated, fertilized, and seeded. It was expected to be completed by October and handed over to John Messick for management.

Aerial photo taken by Pat Thomas before he landed his aircraft on the landing strip, bottom right. Courtesy of Leslie Thomas Gayle.

As soon as the airstrip was operational, Leslie recalls how her dad went to check it out. "He and my boyfriend, now husband, flew over a couple of times to assess the quasi-airstrip. Dad thought it looked pretty good so, the next thing my husband knew, Dad was putting the plane down in front of the house. At touchdown, it almost flipped over because the sand was so soft but miraculously, they landed safely!"

---

[7] Ken Cosgrove folder, Old Baldy Foundation online archive.

Yet even earlier in the decade, another Generator Society pilot chose to make even more daring landings. "Before we built our house in '75," Jeff Cosgrove recalls, "my dad would land us on the beach at the Point and then taxi the plane behind a dune. We would pitch a tent and camp right there for a few days. We were the only people on the island."

Dena Cosgrove, Jeff Cosgrove's wife, recalls those beach landings as less of a fun adventure and more of a traumatic experience. "I flew with my father-in-law one time when he landed on the beach. I wanted to walk home after that, instead of getting back in the plane. Every time he offered to fly us to Bald Head Island after that, I said 'no.' Landing on the beach was quite an experience."

Aerial photo of the Point. Photo courtesy of BHI Limited.

While some of the pilots' family members shared Dena's deep reservations about flying, others fell in love with the experience, going on to obtain their own pilot licenses. Such was the case for all three of the Thomas children and Ken Cosgrove's wife, Eleanor.

In addition to the thrill of flying, it was undeniably convenient. "The airstrip made life a little easier for Dad to come and go," Leslie Thomas explains. "He would keep groceries and his clothing in the plane so he could easily jump to BHI instead of having to drive, work around the tides to get into the creek, and load our stuff into our truck on the island."

According to Harper Peterson, the landing strip and the golf course both played into the draw of Bald Head Island. Yet after just seven years of use, the airstrip closed in August 1984[8] when the next phase of development began, causing the property to be divided into lots.

Members of the Bald Head Aviators

Dr. Thad Wester
Dr. F. A. Berne
Mr. Charles D. Young
Dr. Eugene Douglas
Mr. Robert C. Hayes
Dr. Kenneth Cosgrove
Mr. Earl Congdon
Mr. David Rawley, Jr.
Mr. Warren N. Pollock
Dr. Dick Akers
Mr. Fred Abernathy
Drs. R. W. & Barbara Kitchel
Mr. Phil Calton
Mr. Frank Smith
Mr. John Thomas, Jr.
Mr. Reid Page
Mr. Bynum Tudor

[8] Pat Thomas, from an unpublished story, private collection.

The First Homes

Chapter 8
Named by Necessity

There were four things every family needed on Bald Head Island in the 1970s: food, a generator, fuel, and a portable handheld CB radio.

The CB (short for Citizens' Band radio), long used by truck drivers and popularized by the 1975 hit song "Convoy," served as the only mode of communication on the island and with the mainland. Although the Bald Head Inn installed a single telephone line during those early years, it was reserved for emergency use only.

Operating the CB was simple and its reach was immediate, but it wasn't private. Anyone with a CB tuned to the same radio frequency could listen in and comment on what was being shared. Precisely because of this fact, it was a confusing jumble of voices until they could identify who was speaking. So, to remedy the problem, most of the Generator Society families named their houses and used those names as their CB "handles."

Billie Jean Berne offers an example of how it worked, using her familiar welcome greeting: "This is Skylark, here for the weekend. Who's here? Over."

The Old Boat House by Marina Baskakova.

Chapter 9
The Old Boat House
(Thomas "Buck" and Becky Bunn)

Intrigued by the boat shed situated on a ridge at the northern tip of the proposed development near Frying Pan Shoals, Buck and Becky Bunn purchased it and two lots for approximately $25,000 in 1972. Originally built in 1914 for the Life Saving Service, the *Old Boat House*[9] was in desperate need of renovations.

In the beginning, they didn't have indoor plumbing, and even the outhouse wasn't properly secured. But soon Buck and their son Lee, who was about sixteen years old at the time, built an indoor bathroom and connected their generator to the water pump, the stove, and the refrigerator. Because the generator was so loud, however, they frequently opted to cook over a Coleman stove and rely on ice chests to keep the food cold.

Buck and Lee did about half of the construction work themselves. In addition to the bathroom, they replaced damaged shingles and walls, and insulated the entire house, even under the floor—once they could get to it.

The floor of the main room, where the hulls of wooden boats had long before been tarred to make them water-resistant, still retained a thick layer of the black, sticky substance. It was so deep that the duo had to use shovels to remove it before installing a subfloor and durable carpet. As the carpet installers unrolled the bolt of material into

---

[9] *The Old Boat House* later caught the attention of artist Bob Timberlake as well, who made a painting of it. Mr. Timberlake kindly sold the first of the 250 limited-edition prints to the Bunn family.

the main room, they shared their experience of getting their truck stuck several times on the sandy roads that led to the Bunn residence.[10]

Buck considered Bald Head Island a welcome respite from his busy career as an attorney with Hatch, Little & Bunn (the law firm his father had established) and a former member of the House of Representatives (1963–1969). He enjoyed fishing at the Point with Thad Wester and exploring with his family. They discovered white owls that nested at the top of the lighthouse and all manner of seashells along the beach. "My daughter found a horse conch that must have been three feet long," he recalls.

As development of the island continued, the Bunns were forced to move the house to the end of Sea Lavender Court because its original location was smack dab in the path of a planned road. And though the home was moved, the amenities weren't upgraded. Buck recalls primitive evenings around kerosene lamps and Coleman stoves before trundling off to bed.

Buck sold the house just two years later, in 1974, when he and Becky divorced and were dividing property. "Afterward, my second wife, Patricia, and I [made] annual trips to the island, staying weekends at the inn," he concludes.

---

[10] Thomas Bunn, interview by Kim Gottshall, 2009; and from responses to Bill Berne's questionnaire distributed in 2005.

Skylark by Marina Baskakova.

Chapter 10
Skylark
(Bill and Billie Jean Berne)
Architect: Stanmar Homes and Bill Berne

When selecting their homesite in 1973, the Bernes opted for the shade and varied wildlife of the forest over the perpetual sun and sand of the beach. In their early thirties with three young boys, the couple hired a contractor and eagerly anticipated the completion of their island getaway. They envisioned a simple yet inviting place to unwind after a busy week of building a new medical practice and corralling energetic youngsters.

Yet despite their best-laid plans, problems quickly arose. After the first and then the second contractor quit over the difficulty of transporting materials, they hired a third contractor … who promptly took their money and fled the country. It was at that point that Bill decided to build the house himself.

"I thought he was crazy," Billie Jean recalls, "but I have to give him credit. He did it."

Bill often worked at his medical practice in Lumberton before driving to Southport, catching a boat ride to the island, and working on the house until the sun set. After catching some sleep, he would rise early the next morning, return to Lumberton, and repeat the cycle.

On the weekends, his entire family joined him at Bald Head Island. The boys, due to their ages, were tasked with picking up nails and stacking lumber as Bill and Billie Jean handled the more difficult jobs, all of them enjoying their time together. Of course, that doesn't mean they didn't experience challenging and frustrating moments. In addition to the manual labor of building a house, they also had to haul water to bathe in, cook over camp stoves, and light kerosene lanterns at night. Billie Jean remembers one particular evening when, after tucking the boys into their sleeping bags, she gratefully sank onto her military-style cot. As she turned off the flashlight and stretched out, half the cot collapsed. With her head and torso dangling diagonally, she began to laugh hysterically. "I could not stop laughing. I heard one of the boys whisper, 'Is she okay, Daddy?' and I thought to myself, *I have a perfectly beautiful home in Lumberton with electricity, air conditioning, a swimming pool, and no mosquitoes. Everything that I could possibly want. Why am I here, God?*"

It would have been easy to give up and quit like the contractors, but the Bernes persevered, choosing to see humor and adventure in each situation.

Such was the case when a real estate agent stopped by with two couples who wanted to tour the house for ideas. It was still under construction but Bill, who was working alone that day, agreed. As the men walked around outside, the women meandered through the interior. It soon became apparent to Bill, who was wearing construction coveralls, that the women believed him to be the contractor. After murmuring to each other how strange it was that the wall separating the kitchen from the living room didn't extend all the way to the ceiling, one of them turned to Bill and asked, "Why would they do that?" Playing the part, he responded, "I don't know, ma'am. I just do what the boss tells me."

Bill and Billie Jean ultimately completed the house and used it almost every weekend—spring through fall—until 1995, when they sold it in order to build a new house. Once that new house was built, they lived full-time on the island until 2007, each of them holding active leadership roles in the community.

Looking back, Bill describes their experiences as being *Robinson Crusoe*, *The Swiss Family Robinson*, and *Tom Sawyer* all rolled into one. With little or no maintenance support for malfunctioning generators, frozen pipes, and a multitude of other issues, he concludes, "You'd better not have it on BHI if you didn't know how to fix it."

Raccoon Hilton by Marina Baskakova.

Chapter 11
Raccoon Hilton
(Thad and Lee Wester)
Architect: Stanmar Homes

During Thad and Lee Wester's preliminary visit to BHI, it was the island's maritime forest—not its ocean views—that beckoned to them and solidified the sale. Uninterested in their requisite beachfront lot (which they eventually traded for additional property along the fairway), they selected a homesite among the trees beside the golf course.

Throughout 1973 a succession of contractors bowed out of the Wester project, ultimately causing Thad and Lee to oversee the delivery and assembly of the prefab home themselves. Their daughter Ginny was a young teen at the time and recalls how she and her siblings were frequently taken out of school to spend long weekends on the island, building the house one wall at a time. "We knew it was time to get to work in the morning when we were woken up by Daddy starting the generator," she says.

They slept on cots in the living room, surrounded by stacks of paneling waiting to be hung, and enjoyed uninterrupted coastal breezes through the open windows. They used a piece of plywood for a kitchen table and hung sheets around the bathroom for privacy. And although plumbing had been installed, they had no running water.

They did have clean water, though. A lagoon had recently been dug in their backyard, providing water "so pristine and clear you could see all the way to the bottom." In those early days they hauled buckets out to the lagoon and back to flush the toilet, but later,

Ginny and her sister simply considered the lagoon to be their own private swimming pool, which provided them the freedom to skinny dip on occasion.

For the Westers, the home-building process transitioned from a mere adventure into a treasured heritage.

Happy House by Marina Baskakova.

Chapter 12
Happy House
(Pat and Jo Thomas)

While living in High Point, Pat and Jo Thomas heard about Bald Head Island from a friend and decided to visit. The *Old Boat House* caught their eye and soon they purchased it from Buck and Becky Bunn. Their daughter Leslie was excited that the Bunns' aging Volkswagen Beetle was included in the deal. "I learned to drive in that Bug," she recalls.

Situated on the corner of Muscadine Wynd and S. Bald Head Wynd (the Bunns had been forced to move it from its original location), the home quickly became their "Happy House." They launched into renovations, picking up where the Bunns had left off and installing salvaged stair railings and leaded glass windows from the old North Carolina state capitol.

The upstairs consisted of one large open room, which the children shared as a bedroom for several years. Three windows provided a wonderful cross-breeze—until Pat and Jo installed partitions once the kids became teenagers. While the newfound privacy was welcomed, the lack of air circulation was not. The rooms became uncomfortably hot in the summer after the fans were turned off at night. (For safety reasons, everyone on the island shut off their generators before climbing into bed.)

The house wasn't the only thing that was a challenge to keep cool. "Keeping food cold was a constant battle," Leslie says. "We had several coolers out on the side porch. One was so big, we called it 'the coffin' and that's where we kept all the drinks."

Pat and Jo often brought their entire family to the island … including their four-legged members: a white German Shepherd named Teton and a Basenji named Spook. Pat had purchased the Basenji from a breeder with the hopes of securing a hunting dog. "Lo and behold, the dog had been groomed and trained to be a show dog," Leslie recalls. "She was of no use for hunting and always up to no good!"

One time while at the Point, the dogs were having a glorious time running in the wide-open space … until Spook decided to head over a dune and take off. "She ran and she ran and she ran," Leslie says. "We lost her for two days." Her return was thanks in large part to Pat contacting a boat captain over the CB to get a fish spotter in the air. "My dad, being a pilot, knew that there were pilots that would fly around, looking for schools of fish and then alerting the various fishermen and their commercial boats," she explains. "So a pilot flew over the island and spotted her near Bluff and Middle Islands."

Pat and Jo loved the nature and freedom Bald Head Island afforded. Jo and the kids stayed there all summer each year, with Pat coming down on weekends when he could. "My parents were fun, loving, and they weren't afraid of a challenge," Leslie says.

MilBo Hilton by Marina Baskakova.

Chapter 13
MilBo Hilton
(Bo and Mildred Caperton)
Architect: Stanmar
Contractor: Owen Construction, Banner Elk, North Carolina

Bo and Mildred Caperton bought their lots in 1972 and moved into their home in June 1974. "My grandparents were amazing, as not many people their age would embark on such a primitive adventure for a retirement home," Jeff Caperton states.

Yet even in retirement, Mildred believed in maintaining schedules and routines. "In the mornings, the generator only ran for one or two hours max and then again after a return from the beach for hot showers and appliances to be operational," Jeff says. "You had to be 'on the plan'—there was no place for what you wanted if it wasn't at the right time."

Millie Caperton McVey and her family frequently visited her parents at the MilBo and recalls several occasions when they were the only ones on the island. Although the Bernes, Westers, and Thomases also had homes there, none of them were year-round residents at that time, which ensured periodic isolation.

Much of the Caperton family's time was spent on the beach. "'Amma' loved to take her daily treatment in the ocean every afternoon, swimming half a mile, weather permitting," Jeff recalls. The family also enjoyed fishing, walking along the shore, and digging in the sand. On one occasion they unearthed an old cable spool, which they loaded onto the back of their Jeep and used as a coffee table on the deck.

Since there were no stores on the island,[11] everyone brought food and drinks with them from the mainland. But every once in a while, they ran out of essentials. Kellie Terrell remembers her grandmother placing orders with the grocery store in Southport via the CB radio. The staples would be sent via boat to the island the same day; the bill to be paid later that week. The CB also served as a source of information, one might even say entertainment, as they listened in on the chatter of fishermen and shrimpers.

Ultimately, it was a place for both exploration and relaxation—the realization of a retirement dream.

REMEMBER ...

Mildred and Bo, building their home
On an island so quiet with places to roam.
Generators with power that would come and go.
CBs and jeeps and a pace oh so slow...

... She loved martins and egrets and Pelicans, too.
The fruities at six were her own special brew!
Long walks to the Point and back again,
The grin of delight as she rode the waves in.

... Her straight tee shots and full crab pots,
The card games of nickels of which she won lots!
The turtles, the Chapel, the old Bald Head Inn,
Her fun and good times with family and friends.

And now on this night the breeze echoes her name,
The moon sings alone ... it just isn't the same.

But our mother, grandmother, our wonderful friend,
Your spirit and joy with us will not end.
We will always remember the love that you gave
In the flight of the gull, on the crash of a wave.

   In memory of Mildred Caperton

   —Shelley McVey Boehling
   June 17, 1996

---

[11] A small convenience store would later be available at the marina, but the first official grocery store on the island didn't open until 2001.

Rockhound by Marina Baskakova.

Chapter 14
Rockhound
(Joe and Buris Crowell)

Architect: William O'Cain II
Contractor: Joe Crowell Jr.

Joe Crowell Sr. and his wife, Buris, chose to nestle their house among the trees near the third fairway of the golf course. Their son, Joe Jr., claimed to have "burnt-up" three 150-horsepower motors on his McKee Craft boat during the building process as he shuffled men and materials between Southport and the island.

During one of Buris's mother/daughter trips (which also included three young grandchildren), the lack of a functioning generator didn't deter them from staying the entire week. Ever resourceful, they bathed in the golf course sprinklers, cooked over a gas grill, and obtained drinking water from Bald Head Inn.

Pilot House by Marina Baskakova.

Chapter 15
Pilot House
(Jimmy and Margaret Harper)
Contractor: Walter Sellers

Late one Saturday afternoon, Jimmy Harper stood in his Southport home and, as he was wont to do, gazed across the Cape Fear River to Bald Head Island. It was Easter weekend, and Jimmy and his wife had opted to celebrate in Southport rather than at their second home on the island.

"I saw a glow in the sky and commented that it looked like somebody's house may be burning," he recalls. As he would soon learn, it was the garage of his own Pilot House.

This occurred in the 1970s before there was a fire department nearby, so they called for assistance over the CB. As people flocked to help, they stopped at neighbors' homes along the way to make sure they'd heard the call as well.

"We had just sat down to dinner when we saw an International Harvester Scout come around with its horn blaring and lights flashing," Leslie Thomas says. "Someone yelled, 'Did you hear? Get your buckets. The Harper's house is on fire!' So of course everybody jumped up to help. I'll never forget that!"

Ginny Wester recalls that evening as well. "We had just turned off the generator and sat down to one of our typical evening meals of steak and hash browns when the island security officer banged on the front door to notify us."

Approximately forty people raced down Stede Bonnet Road to discover the Harper's garage engulfed in flames, with tongues of fire beginning to lick at the corner of the house. According to those who were there, Thad Wester formed an old-fashioned bucket brigade, sending half the group to fill trash cans with water from the lagoon at the eleventh fairway and encouraging the other half to dig trenches to prevent the fire from spreading to the vegetation.

Smaller buckets were then filled with water and passed up to the second-story roof of the house, where a handful of fearless men poured water down the sides of the smoldering walls. A few men climbed ladders and used axes to knock off flaming pieces of lumber to prevent further spread, while other volunteers entered the house and began tossing furniture outside in an attempt to save some of the Harper's belongings.

"My house is a monument to hard work and good neighbors," Jimmy says. "That spontaneous effort saved it from destruction. I'll never forget what those brave volunteers did."

It was later determined that the fire was caused by gasoline that had landed on the pilot light when visiting guests were attempting to refill the generator.

After the house was repaired, Bill Berne presented Jimmy and Margaret with the First Disaster Award—a simple plaque engraved only with the letters "FD," which hung prominently in their *Pilot House* living room for many years.

The Seven C's by Marina Baskakova.

Chapter 16
The Seven C's
(Ken and Eleanor Cosgrove)
Architect: Emery Jackson, Hendersonville, North Carolina
Contractor: Joe Crowell Jr.

In the 1960s, long before Bald Head Island was developed, the Cosgroves would camp near the abandoned Coast Guard station (the future Bunn/Thomas home). With a love for the island firmly established, it was only natural that they would build a home there when the opportunity arose in 1975. They named it the *Seven C's* in honor of their seven family members.

As it had been for all the first families, Ken found himself immersed in a massive self-improvement project. "It was a very special time and as amazing as it sounds, I actually became quite a passable electrician and plumber because of it," he explains.

Once the house was complete, new adventures awaited.

"We were kind of brave to take our newborn babies down to BHI," Jeff's wife, Dena Cosgrove, reflects. "Trying to rely on a generator that didn't work all the time, cars that broke down on the other side of the island, and [not being able to] see a thing along Federal Road—the darkest place in the whole wide world because the tree canopy covered the entire road. There were no cell phones and we usually didn't have a flashlight because we were young and unprepared. But Frank Poole was our pediatrician in Raleigh so that was a great comfort to know he and his son, Jim, also a pediatrician, were usually there on the weekends as well."

Neptune by Marina Baskakova.

Chapter 17
Neptune
(Charlie and Patricia Young)
Contractor: Walter Sellers

Broad-shouldered and standing six feet four, Charlie Young was a man who commanded attention when he entered a room. "He couldn't whisper if he tried," Patricia recalls, "but he had a gentle way of saying things." Ken Cosgrove concurs: "He was a big man—kinda like John Wayne—and he had this big, deep voice."

"Charlie and I hadn't been dating for too long when he told me that he owned an island," she says. "I thought, *Yeah, sure. He's funny … maybe a little crazy.* Turned out he did own an island! He had just bought Middle Island and had a house (*Neptune*) on BHI."

Charlie had long enjoyed fishing and hunting wild hogs on the island, beginning in the 1960s. It was only natural, then, that he would purchase property when the development began, selecting South Beach as the location for a house that afforded stunning views of both the Atlantic Ocean and the Cape Fear River.

He and his brother Richard painted the home that initially sat on a bluff near today's Bald Head Club. However, erosion eventually led the *Neptune* to be moved back … at least twice.[12] Each of the bedrooms featured large sliding doors with screens, which were left open at night so the ocean breeze could sweep through.

---

[12] Accounts vary; some state it was moved twice, while another source claims it was three times.

Charlie and Patricia stayed at the house almost every weekend, spending a lot of time there with Charlie's brother Richard and his wife, Vicki. All of them considered it a welcome retreat and a great place for the children to explore. "Cooper, Richard and Vicki's son, was born in 1977 and he tells people that he has been going to the island since 'pre-birth!'" Patricia laughs.

One weekend, David invited a friend along. "He was about seven years old at the time," Patricia recalls. "We all watched a movie that had David and his friend crying salty tears by the time it ended." After tucking them into their sleeping bags, Charlie and Patricia turned off the generator and went to bed. "I woke up in the middle of the night and could barely move because there were four bodies in the bed. It was so sweet."

The Sandfiddler by Marina Baskakova.

Chapter 18
The Sandfiddler
(Billy and Charlotte Dunlap; Bobby and Frankie McMahan; Mrs. Dunlap—Billy & Frankie's Mom)

Architect: Bob McMahan (Billy's brother-in-law)

Raleigh residents Billy and Charlotte Dunlap learned about Bald Head Island from their friend and fellow physician Frank Poole. After visiting the island in the early 1970s, they decided it was the perfect place to build a vacation getaway.

So, for approximately $25,000, they purchased a beachfront lot with high dunes. Despite the natural buffer, Billy decided to build the house well away from the beach, toward the back of the property. Even so, his mother asked, "Don't you think this lot is a little close to the water?" But Billy wasn't at all concerned, thinking he had taken all the precautions necessary.

So, with help from friends and relatives, they built *The Sand Fiddler*, named after the small crabs commonly found in the Bald Head Island sand. With minimal professional help, the Dunlaps built a rustic, if rather primitive, dwelling. With its unfinished walls, kerosene heaters, and wood stove for cooking, it was more akin to camping in the wilderness than vacationing at a beachfront resort.

"Living on Bald Head Island in the early years taught you how to cope," Charlotte says.

This phase of construction lasted so long that their son Marshall thought they would be living in a half-finished house forever. But as time went on, more and more features were added until the building was complete.

It featured four upstairs bedrooms plus four bunk beds on the ground floor for the children. Gas lanterns provided light and a wood stove heated the entire house; the generator powered the dishwasher, washer and dryer, and stereo.

One of their most unusual appliances was a gas-powered refrigerator. Now commonly used for camping and other remote activities, it was at that time a novelty. Small and compact, it did a good job of keeping the food cold but could only make about one full tray of ice per day.

Despite all the amenities, life on the island remained more primitive than the mainland and was fraught with challenges, including the relentless tides. Billy's mother had been right (as mothers often are): their house was too close to the ocean. When it finally reached the point that they could fish from their porch, they moved the house back.

Whenever Billy, Charlotte, Marshall, and Wick went to the island, they were always accompanied by Billy's mother, sister, brother-in-law (Bob, the contractor for the house), and their children. This extended family spent every Thanksgiving Marshall can remember on the island and often returned a few weeks later to ring in the new year, at which time the adults would get into all manner of mischief while the kids and their island friends got into trouble of their own.

When Marshall was twenty-six, he finally spent a long weekend there by himself. At the time, the house had been unlivable due to beach erosion and was set to be moved back for the second time. It was so far out on the beach it resembled an oil rig standing in the middle of the open surf.

Given that all the power and utilities in the house were unhooked, Marshall opted to sleep on the roof, just like he had with his friends as a teenager. Hearing the sound of the waves crashing against the sand and staring up into the radiant night sky, untouched by smog or light pollution, made it seem like the island was a world of its own.

After the Dunlaps moved the house the second time, they continued to enjoy the benefits it offered. Billy and Charlotte divorced in the early 1990s but maintained an amicable relationship. Charlotte received *The Sandfiddler* in the settlement but always let Billy use the house whenever he wanted.

Yet moving the house away from the breakers—twice—still wasn't enough to fully protect it. Heavy winds and rain from a ravaging storm caused the roof to cave in, condemning the house. It was a sad and untimely end—but to Billy, *The Sandfiddler* represented twenty-seven years of fun and adventure.

C Turtle by Marina Baskakova.

Chapter 19
C Turtle
(Earl and Kitty Congdon)
Contractor: Bill Owen, Banner Elk, North Carolina
Designers: Bill Owen (and the Congdons)

It was March 28, 1975, and Earl and Kitty looked forward to getting their appliances hooked up and the carpet laid. They left High Point early that morning accompanied by Karen and David Penley (just back from their honeymoon) as well as Troy Beddington (their carpet layer) and three members of his crew, arriving at BHI during early high tide. Their contractor, Bill Owen, arrived later to hook up their gas refrigerator and stove.

Knowing that the carpet would take all day to put down, Kitty planned to feed the installers dinner. So, after seeing to her own things, Kitty went to the kitchen that afternoon to check on the status of the appliances. That's when she learned that the stove in the box was an electric model. With only gas lines available, she wondered how she would feed the hungry workers and her family.

After rummaging through their stored possessions, they managed to unearth a gas grill and two full tanks of propane. That worked well for cooking the steak and potatoes, but as for heating up the rolls, a bit more creativity was required.

Earl started the generator—"it was too new to malfunction," Kitty observes—and connected it to the dishwasher. "The drying cycle made a good roll heater," she laughs.

That evening, as they enjoyed their meal by the light of oil lamps, they didn't realize their experience that day would set the stage for countless days and nights to come.

Captain Charlie's Station by Marina Baskakova. This property is featured on the cover of this book.

Chapter 20
Captain Charlie's Station
(Robin and Barbara Hayes)

Four friends purchased *Captain Charlie's Station* from CCFC when the company went into receivership in 1977: Robin and Barbara Hayes, Richard Thigpen, and Jeff Mullin. They immediately set about restoring the first of the three cottages that comprise the complex located at the southeasternmost point of South Beach.

The complex at one time also included the Cape Fear Lighthouse, which operated from 1903 to 1958. It was the third lighthouse constructed on the island, not to be confused with the much older Bald Head Lighthouse (Old Baldy) that operated from 1817 to 1935 along West Beach and still stands today.[13] The two lighthouses differed from each other most notably by their outward appearance. The 161-foot-tall Cape Fear Lighthouse featured an airy, skeletal frame resembling a fire tower, whereas Old Baldy, standing at only 110 feet, represents an imposing octagonal brick-and-stucco bulwark.

The namesake of *Captain Charlie's Station* was Charles Norton Swan, the first keeper of the Cape Fear Lighthouse. Assuming the position at the age of thirty, he had already established himself as a well-respected mariner, having previously served as a seaman on the three-masted schooner *The Water Witch* and as the captain of the *Frying Pan*

---

[13] The very first Bald Head Lighthouse operated from 1794 to 1813, when the U.S. government tore it down due to beach erosion. The Old Baldy we see today replaced that original structure. Abby Overton, "Bald Head Island History," Old Baldy Foundation, 2020, https://www.oldbaldy.org/history.

Shoals Lightship.[14] His family lived part of the year with him on the island in one of the cottages and the rest of the year in the Southport home Charlie had built next door to his good friend and fellow lightkeeper James Henry (Sonny) Dosher, the keeper of Old Baldy.

Not long after the Hayeses and friends purchased *Captain Charlie's Station*, Richard tragically drowned in a rip current while visiting the island. Bereft, the Hayes and Mullin families never returned, eventually selling *Captain Charlie's* to the Mitchells when they took ownership of Bald Head Island in the early 1980s. The cottages were then turned into vacation rentals, which continue to be available to island guests.

---

[14] Lightships were boats outfitted with a bright light and moored near dangerous water areas to warn sea captains; this was for when traditional lighthouses couldn't be constructed due to the inhospitable terrain—and before the invention of automated flashing buoys.

Tree House by Marina Baskakova.

Chapter 21
Tree House
(Frank and Harriet Poole)
Architect: Bill Dodge
Contractors: Lee Willick & Sons; Bobby McMahan; Tom Dosher & John Jordan; Robert Franklin

When Bill Henderson visited the home of Frank and Harriet Poole in 1972, he presented them with pictures of Bald Head Island and offered a two-lot package for $21,000. They accepted and became the 100th buyer.

Six years later, in May 1978, the first pilings were inserted on Lot 688, but by January the house was only 30 percent finished. Part of the delay may have been due to Frank changing the house plans (turning cathedral ceilings into a second story and adding separate balconies to each of the four upstairs bedrooms, for example), but it was also because of the revolving bevy of contractors. By April 1979, Frank finally took over.

Every weekend Frank exchanged his white physician's coat for a one-piece mechanic's suit and got to work. Harriet regularly worked alongside him but preferred to be the self-proclaimed "look for-er" and "go get-er."

Originally consisting of two 1400-square-foot homes connected by decking, the Poole's complex was so close to the trees that it appeared to rest in them, giving rise to the name *Tree House*. With the eventual addition of a workshop, it became, as Ken Cosgrove put it, "three little bungalows tied together by a porch."

"Truly, Frank has created this wonderful house with his mind and hands," Harriet says. "He'd make lists and draw plans each night in Raleigh, then we'd come on the weekend and he'd execute them."

Frank possessed many admirable qualities; he was orderly, structured, compassionate, fun loving … and frugal. Rather than rent the barge to haul a single, full load of bricks, for example, he instead chose to ferry them across with him, two whiskey boxes at a time. In addition, he avoided purchasing brand-new building supplies whenever possible.

Once, an acquaintance handed him the key to a building slated to be gutted and said, "Take all you want." So Frank did, driving away with sinks, brass handles, hinges, cabinets, doors, and heavy paneling. On many occasions, he went dumpster diving. "Whenever Dad got to the island, he immediately got in the Jeep to go scour the dumpsters of the new construction sites," James Poole recalls.

And, of course, he was a beachcomber who delighted in reusing and recycling items long before it became a national habit. When the Bald Head Inn was scheduled to be dismantled in 1988, for example, Frank obtained permission to remove materials from the partially submerged building just before its demolition. He and Harriet worked at low tide to salvage a bookcase, a bathroom sink, and imported tile. Frank, with hammer and wedge in hand, feverishly popped off pieces of tile as waves crashed against him, regularly knocking him down.

Despite Frank's valiant efforts to reduce costs, "the house, the deck—it all got bigger and bigger," Harriet recalls. "It was like throwing money down a deep, bottomless well."

Yet it was money—and time—both Frank and Harriet considered well spent.

Upon arrival at the island, they—like so many of their neighbors—primed the water pump, cranked up the generator, and pumped 500 gallons of water to a holding tank so they would have running water during their stay. Before that system was set up, however, families had to rely on old-fashioned hand pumps. Harriet recalls the day Charlie Young happened by, saw Frank installing a hand pump, and stopped to offer assistance. "Charlie pounded away for a while . . . until the head flew off his hammer. Thank goodness he wasn't hurt! After that, he just slowed up and waved as he went by."

For heat, Frank and Harriet bought a wood stove, and for hot water, they installed a solar water system—another example of Frank being ahead of the times. Once electricity reached the island, Frank installed an electric water heater and created an automatic watering system for their landscaping.

"Bald Head Island is sort of like the Belgian Congo when it comes to plant growth," Harriet says. "After Hurricane Diana, our tall trees were killed from the swirling salt air, which allowed the underbrush to really thrive. Frank had to literally carve our yard out of the vines. But he loved doing it."

In fact, Frank built a relaxing oasis in their yard featuring a meandering brick walkway with many azalea, oleander, and hydrangea bushes framing it on either side. It was still the pioneer years, after all, long before homeowners were limited by how much they could prune and plant.

One thing Frank *couldn't* remedy back then—and what continues to be an issue today on the island—was the high level of iron in the water. "According to our doctor, it was better than Geritol," Harriet says.[15]

Tree House instructions for guests.

Nestled in among trunks, branches, and leaves, the Poole's home looked every bit the *Tree House*.

---

[15] A water treatment center wasn't installed on the island until 1997. Today, the water still isn't considered good by many people, who continue to drink bottled water there.

Cindy Poole Roberts recalls her father's evening routine following a long day of work: "At five o'clock he would pour his 'party' and sit on the tiny second-story porch of his workshop, which was only big enough for one chair, and look across the fairway toward the beach."

Yet Frank didn't isolate himself for long, since he and Harriet also enjoyed entertaining guests.

"Dad loved meeting new people on the boat, especially if they were foreigners, and would always invite them over to the house," Cindy says. "Mom was such a great sport! In Raleigh, she was the social butterfly, not Dad, so I think she loved when he did this. They were always having guests over to the house."

One of those guests was Ann Cathcart, who particularly remembers being greeted by Frank one rainy evening. "Frank met me at the door and said, 'I'll take your coat.' So I handed him my rain jacket and watched as he walked over to the wall, took out a hammer and a big old nail, pounded the nail into the wall, and hung my coat. I thought, *Well, okay then!* That just epitomized Frank Poole."

Harriet recalls hosting other memorable events, such as dinners with exposed rafters and insulation, and plastic flapping over the holes for windows. "But no one complained; we had lots of laughs and fun."

Van Eure agrees. "We just found so much joy at their house," she says. "It was like a big playpen; it was the essence of fun there."

Blue Crab by Marina Baskakova.

Chapter 22
Blue Crab
(Cash and Irma Caroon)
Contractor: Custom Crib, Long Beach, North Carolina

Prior to the construction of the *Blue Crab*, Cash decided to clear the property himself using a chainsaw. Situated along the golf course and overlooking a lagoon, the property "was nothing but a maze of trees and vines that we couldn't walk through," Irma recalls.

All was going well until the day Cash's chainsaw unexpectedly bounced off a vine and cut his face. "Suddenly Cash hollered that he couldn't see," Irma remembers. "We knew none of those who already had homes on the island [but] I ran to the Jeep and called for help over the CB. Within minutes, island folks came from all directions."

Cash was rushed to Dosher Memorial Hospital in Southport, where he made a full recovery. "I hate to imagine what the outcome would have been if it hadn't been for those caring people who are now our dear friends," Irma concludes.

Hickory Nut by Marina Baskakova.

Chapter 23
Hickory Nut
(Harry and Elva Schmulling)

The Schmullings utilized the same type of gravity water tank that Bobby McMahan (Billy Dunlap's brother-in-law) had invented. Situated in the attic, its operation, although simple enough in theory, nevertheless often caused confusion for members of Harry and Elva's family.

In order to work properly, the water tank's faucet, the outdoor water supply faucet, and the house faucet had to be used in a certain order. However, in the Schmulling home, it was not uncommon for faucets that were to be shut off be left on, and vice versa, causing water to unexpectedly pour out of the wrong location. Inevitably, an unsuspecting family member would be deluged with water until someone could shut off the generator and stop the waterfall.

The Schmullings couldn't wait for electricity to arrive on the island.

Sand Dollar by Marina Baskakova.

Chapter 24
Sand Dollar
(Reddy and Bippie Grubbs)
Architect: Hunter Smith
Contractor: Walter Sellers

While it was customary for property owners on Bald Head Island to receive a crash course in construction, the Grubbs also received cooking lessons. During fishing season, the building crew adjusted their hours earlier so they could put in a full eight-hour shift and still have time to cast their rods before it got dark. These skilled fishermen shared their catches with the Grubbs and taught them how to clean and cook the fish, particularly the plentiful bluefish.

The Grubbs also did a fair amount of house painting. Reddy put the boys, Mike and Steve, to work coating the exterior while he, Bippie, and Nan painted the interior.

The house, once complete, served as a welcome respite not just for their family but for strangers as well. Nan Grubbs recalls one evening when she and two friends heard a knock at the door and were surprised to discover two strangers standing on the porch. The men explained that their sailboat had run aground during an East Coast race and, as they walked the beach searching for assistance, the only light they could find was that illuminating the *Sand Dollar*.

"I don't know how our light could have helped them," Nan muses. "The generator was out and we were only burning candles!"

Young One by Marina Baskakova.

Chapter 25
Young One—Middle Island
(Charlie and Patricia Young)

Charlie Young and his younger half brother Richard acquired Middle Island in 1978 for less than $400,000. Charlie and Richard then established Young Realty Co., Inc., naming their children and spouses as shareholders. "All of the property on Middle Island was owned by the Company and we all shared in the benefits and expenses, which is why you will see 'The Young Family' on all of the donations and land gifts," Pat explains.[16] The land and house (*Neptune*) on Bald Head Island, however, were owned solely by Charles.

As owners of Middle Island, Charles and his family faced the daunting task of clearing future homesites of dense thickets of vines. Rather than manually cutting the extensive creepers, Charlie brought in goats to do the job—at one point almost twenty of them. To keep them contained and to restrict human access—especially during the week when he and Patricia lived in Charlotte—he erected a gate.

When Patricia discovered an orphaned kid, she and Charlie took the helpless goat back to Charlotte with them, where they nursed it back to health. Sweet Pea, as the kid was affectionately called, provided plenty of entertainment. "I would feed her a bottle in the

---
[16] The Young Company sold their last piece of property on Middle Island in 2021.

morning and then place her in the dog pen in the backyard," Patricia says. "Our house adjoined a golf course, and as the golfers were getting ready to tee off, she would cry. It was funny to watch as they looked all around to see where it was coming from." Once Sweet Pea was able to eat solid food, she was reunited with her herd.

When the goats eventually began eating tree leaves, Charlie hired a goat herder to remove them. The herder's dog chased and pinned them to the ground, one goat at a time, until the herder successfully roped them all and led them into a pen on wheels. They were then loaded onto the barge and delivered to a goat farm on the mainland.

Without there being a paved road connecting Federal Road to Middle Island, accessing the island often caused an adrenaline rush. "You could get as far as *Captain Charlie's* without a problem but then it turned into really deep sand by the old generator house. You had to have four-wheel drive and you had to drive in reverse to get across; there was no way to do it facing forward," Patricia recalls.

Middle Island opened up slowly in stages, selling only two lots a year for ten years. The first person to purchase property there was Mr. Capel, who, in an effort to remedy the road situation, brought a truck full of rug pieces from his rug store and dumped them over the sand. Charles and Patricia soon built a house there, naming it *Young One*, and fellow Bald Head Island homeowners Ken and Eleanor Cosgrove also built a house.

Like Bald Head Island, Middle Island was powered by generators until electricity arrived in the 1980s, a fact that didn't deter visitors. "We moved to *Young One* and always had a house full of family and/or guests," Patricia recalls. The Youngs considered adding a pool and tennis court to their house—perhaps in an effort to help entertain their constant flow of visitors—but ultimately decided to install the amenities in a central location for all the residents of Middle Island to enjoy.

Charles's affection for Middle Island was apparent to everyone. "He loved that island like nobody's business," Ken Cosgrove recalls. Patricia Young agrees. "If he said it once, he must have said it a thousand times … 'The island comes first.' He was the driving force behind everything that happened." This included the planting of hundreds of native trees, mostly live oaks, and some dogwoods. "He also planted many Japanese black pines because he loved the way they shaped themselves in the salt-air winds of the island," Patricia says. "It was a labor of love."

Hilltop by Marina Baskakova.

Chapter 26
Hilltop
(Bynum Tudor)
Architect: Ben Gross
Contractor: Custom Crib, Long Beach, North Carolina

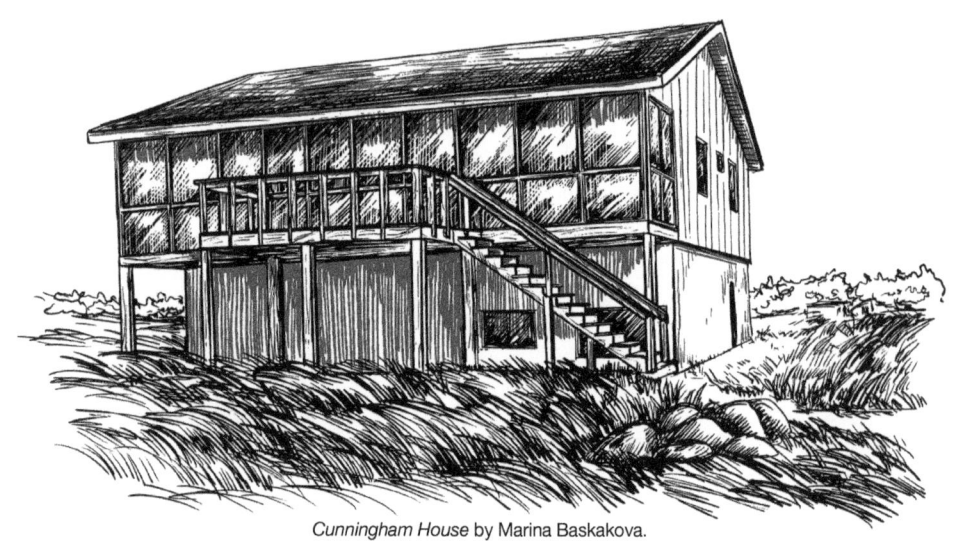

Cunningham House by Marina Baskakova.

Chapter 27
Cunningham House
(Bill and Pat Cunningham)
Contractor: C. W. Joyner of Ocean Isle Beach, North Carolina

PART III: THE EXPANSION

"We are excited about the future of Bald Head Island and ... working with all of you to sensibly develop a place of such inherent natural beauty."
—BHI Limited welcome letter to property owners

Chapter 28
Bald Head Island Property Owners Association (BHI POA)

Even though the Arab–Israeli War was fought half a world away, it nevertheless directly affected Bald Head Island—and all of America. Because the United States supported Israel, Arab-led OPEC (Organization of Petroleum Exporting Countries) imposed an oil embargo on the country from 1973 to 1974.[17]

Suddenly faced with increased gas prices, fuel shortages, and an economic downturn, Carolina Cape Fear Corporation began to struggle. "I still believe the threat to our economy and the difficulty of travel following OPEC's decision was a major factor in stopping the development of BHI in 1974," says Gene Douglas.

Generator Society members also felt the pinch. They faced long lines at the gas pump before heading to the island and increased expenses for almost everything they needed to take with them, including the fuel to operate their generators (especially diesel).

Billie Jean Berne shares yet another cause for development delays: the Sierra Club.

Known for its grassroots environmental preservation efforts, the Sierra Club, along with the Conservation Council of North Carolina, sought to halt further Bald Head Island development. Primary among their concerns were sewage runoff jeopardizing wildlife habitats and pesticides damaging the ecology. The state of North Carolina, which years prior had lost out to CCFC in the bid for the island and which was also concerned about developmental repercussions, often delayed or denied permits. In an effort to appease all parties, CCFC donated 9,000 acres (three-quarters of the entire island) to the state for use as a nature preserve in return for the right to install a marina. Later, members of the BHI Conservancy would help to ensure the proper ecological balance of that land, as well as of its beaches.

When the Sierra Club and the Conservation Council of North Carolina learned that dredging for the marina had begun without the submission of an environmental impact study by the U.S. Army Corps of Engineers, they took CCFC to court. "They held the original developer up in court until they went into receivership," Billie Jean recalls, "so the lenders took over for a while and all of the amenities that we were promised didn't happen. We were in limbo."

Of course, property owners had always known they had invested in a high-risk project; Carolina Cape Fear Corporation had been up-front with them about that fact. But such knowledge doesn't prevent frustration when facing the possible loss of your investment.

---

[17] Office of the Historian, "Oil Embargo, 1973–1974," Foreign Service Institute, United States Department of State, accessed February 10, 2022, https://history.state.gov/milestones/1969-1976/oil-embargo.

THE WHITE HOUSE

WASHINGTON

August 29, 1973

Dear Dr. Poole:

The President has asked that I respond to your recent letter regarding the development of Bald Head Island community by the Carolina Cape Fear Corporation.

It is the responsibility of those agencies involved in the Federal navigable waters permit program to fully comply with environmental law and to work with each developer in assuring that the best environmental technology is incorporated into project plans. The Departments of Interior and Army have worked with Mr. W. R. Henderson of the Carolina Cape Fear Corporation and his staff to ensure that the remaining natural resources of Bald Head Island are protected for present and future generations. Mr. Henderson has been most cooperative in his efforts to make the development plan responsive to environmental goals.

In response to a public notice issued on January 29, 1971, announcing that the Carolina Cape Fear Corporation had applied for Department of the Army after-the-fact approval of an existing pier, letters and telegrams from many interested persons were received. Numerous objections were recorded including those of the Department of the Interior and the North Carolina Department of Conservation and Development. Opposing views were also received from local, State and national environmental groups.

The Corps of Engineers prepared a detailed report on the facts pertinent to the application. Based on a thorough review of this report, the permit was denied by the Department of the Army as not being in the public interest for the following reasons:

1. The pier was only the first of several proposed works in navigable waters, each of which would contribute to the alteration of the natural characteristics of the Island.

2. The development of the Island would disrupt a vast fish and wildlife habitat of unique value.

White House response to Frank Poole regarding the development delays on Bald Head Island. (Continued on next page).

- 2 -

3. A serious risk to public safety would be created by locating a large population on the remote Island with no roadway escape in the event of tropical storms or other emergency.

4. The development may impose a burden on the public treasury by future demands for hurricane protection, beach erosion control structures, stabilization of inlets and protection of public utilities.

5. There is no pressing public need for the development.

6. Potential economic loss to the commercial fishing industry through disruption of the adjacent wetlands.

The Carolina Cape Fear Corporation has presented revised plans for development of the Island complex. Following a careful review of these revisions by the Secretary of the Army's staff, and representatives of other agencies, it was determined that within certain conditions the revisions constitute new information sufficient to justify consideration of a revised application. This is the point at which the matter is today.

We appreciate your interest in these matters and are confident that, by working together, governmental agencies and private industry can bring about a better environment.

Sincerely,

Richard M. Fairbanks
Associate Director
Domestic Council

Dr. Robert F. Poole
Glenwood Professional Village
3001 Essex Circle
Raleigh, North Carolina 27608

So, as CCFC fought in the courts and hoped that the nation's recession would turn around quickly, the roughly 100 Bald Head Island property owners decided to advocate for themselves in order to preserve their holdings. A steering committee for the proposed Bald Head Island Property Owners Association (BHI POA) met in February 1975, and all property owners of record were invited to join the Association for $35 annually. The first organizational meeting was held in March—and with the approval of a charter and bylaws, officers were elected and the BHI POA (a.k.a. "POA"") was born.

It was established just in time.

BHI POA board of directors meeting. Photo courtesy of BHI Association's Bald Head Island newsletter, summer 1983. Photographer: Kelly Carlton.

4—The State Port Pilot, Southport, North Carolina, Wednesday, August 30, 1978

Editorials

This Could Do It

From the time Frank Sherrill purchased Bald Head Island in the 1930's until the death of Bill Keziah in the mid-50's there was the local feeling that development of that unique property one day would help bring about the economic salvation of Brunswick County.

In recent years there have been industrial developments that have dwarfed even Bill Keziah's imagination when it came to adding to the county tax base, and while everyone was interested in the future of Bald Head, no longer was it looked upon as a major source for tax revenue.

Recently, while trying to think what we can do here in Southport to take up the slack caused by removal of county offices, suddenly we realized that a full-throttle development of Bald Head Island would more than do the job. We have some facts to prove it.

Five years ago, before the environmentalists had achieved their stranglehold and before the recession had set in, between 75 and 100 persons were employed on the Carolina-Cape Fear staff. These were intelligent, bright and personable people of many talents, and most of them made their home in Southport. As the preservationists zeroed in on their legal battles and the economic pinch began to hurt progress on island development the project came to a halt and attrition set in for staff personnel.

Had it been permitted to continue along the lines of plans designed by the original developers, Bald Head Island would have been the best thing that ever happened economically to Southport. If any combination of circumstances can result in getting this project back on track, it still could be.

Think of the employment it would afford for workers both in the Southport office and on the island. This would much more than compensate for the loss of jobs held until recently by county employees. Think of the traffic which would be created by property owners and prospective purchasers of lots. This would much more than fill the void resulting form loss of people coming to court, to the tax office and to the Department of Social Services.

For the type of visitors who would come here for visits to the island there would be a demand for more overnight accommodations, for expanded restaurants, for gift shops and for other miscellaneous services. We would in practical effect become the gateway for a multimillion dollar resort for which we would be responsible for none of its headaches and could provide at a profit the kind of services which would help give a good reputation to the entire area.

Think about it.

An anonymous letter to the editor of Southport's *State Port Pilot* outlining the ripple effects of CCFC's demise.

Foreclosure proceedings were filed against CCFC in August 1975. By 1976, Builders Investment Group (one of the four lenders backing CCFC) took over the title of the island and created Bald Head Island Corporation. Then, in 1978, Gate City Savings (another of the four lenders) decided to divest itself of its remaining fifty lots. The company's chairman of the board mailed a letter to property owner Earl Congdon, notifying him of the decision and asking Earl to share the information with interested parties.[18] Finally, in 1979, Texas-based Cambridge Properties under the leadership of Walter Davis bought the island from Builders Investment Group and assumed ownership of Bald Head Island Corporation.

One of the most notable changes Mr. Davis made to the island was laying paved roads. Ken Cosgrove recalls the summer Mr. Davis—who reportedly owned a paving company—brought in the equipment. Soon, his company had replaced deep, sandy thoroughfares such as Federal Road with firm, solid pavement.

Throughout these dizzying changes in ownership, the BHI POA worked hard to retain their properties and maintain services on the island. In 1975, the POA represented BHI homeowners before the Board of Equalization & Review, successfully reducing homeowner tax payments by half over the next eight years. In addition, when Builders Investment Group opted to decrease its interest, BHI POA gained the authority to provide and maintain island services such as security and transportation.

Perhaps most importantly, however, the POA saved the developmental premise. This meant that when a property was sold, all existing restrictions were accepted by the buyer. "By maintaining that premise, they were able to hold the development intact, keep the golf course open, and prevent the mass selling off of property, until the economy changed."[19]

---

[18] Perhaps a letter was sent to each of the property owners, but only Mr. Congdon's letter was discovered during the research for this book.

[19] Old Baldy Foundation subject files, Bald Head Island Association, "A Brief History of the Association," page 22, accessed February 16, 2022, https://drive.google.com/drive/folders/14VCUtQ7GTm13UPaw1MVgl2__4uHlwh8w.

Chapter 29
BHI Limited

George and Cynthia Mitchell bought Bald Head Island from Walter Davis (Bald Head Island Corporation) in 1983 and turned it over to their sons Mark and Kent to manage, which they continue to do today. Operating under the corporate entity BHI Limited (a.k.a. "Limited"), the Mitchells immediately began to lay the foundations necessary to reach their long-term development goals.

For many of the long-established Generator Society members accustomed to a relatively autonomous and secluded lifestyle, life as they knew it on Bald Head Island was about to change.

Change, of course, can be a good thing. But change of any kind requires new ways of thinking and acting. And that doesn't always come easily.

> **Statement From Owner**
>
> "On behalf of the Mitchell family, we would like to extend our greetings to the property owners of Bald Head Island. We intend to continue the previous owners' eye to quality in development and concern for preserving the natural beauty of the island.
>
> "We are currently evaluating the needs and requirements of the island for now and for the future. We realize the marina and transportation to and from the island are important issues at this time. We will be studying, with the help of professional consultants, how to best develop and improve the existing conditions.
>
> "Working with the board of directors of the Bald Head Association will be an integral part of our planning process. Any comments or suggestions you might have will always be appreciated. We encourage you to respond to the questionnaire you find in this newsletter.
>
> "We are excited about the future of Bald Head Island and are looking forward to working with all of you to sensibly develop a place of such inherent natural beauty. Bald Head Island is indeed a masterpiece of nature. Our challenge is to preserve that masterpiece for ourselves and for future generations."
>
> "MARK & KENT MITCHELL"

Statement from BHI Limited's owners, Mark & Kent Mitchell.

Originally, the Mitchells intended to develop their entire holding, which was to include the creation of another golf course on the island's interior since those lots didn't hold as much value. But due to environmental and economic considerations, they ultimately decided to preserve those interior areas rather than cut them up with roads and amenities. Residential areas on the island's perimeter, therefore, became their main focus.

To ensure the utmost care was taken, they consulted with world-class experts in community urban design and hired, according to Harper Peterson, "some really strong, talented people."

Donna Ray Mitchell, for example, was selected as the sole member of the island's planning department, and Harold Crouch was the sole member of the construction department. Also established was the island's communication and transportation

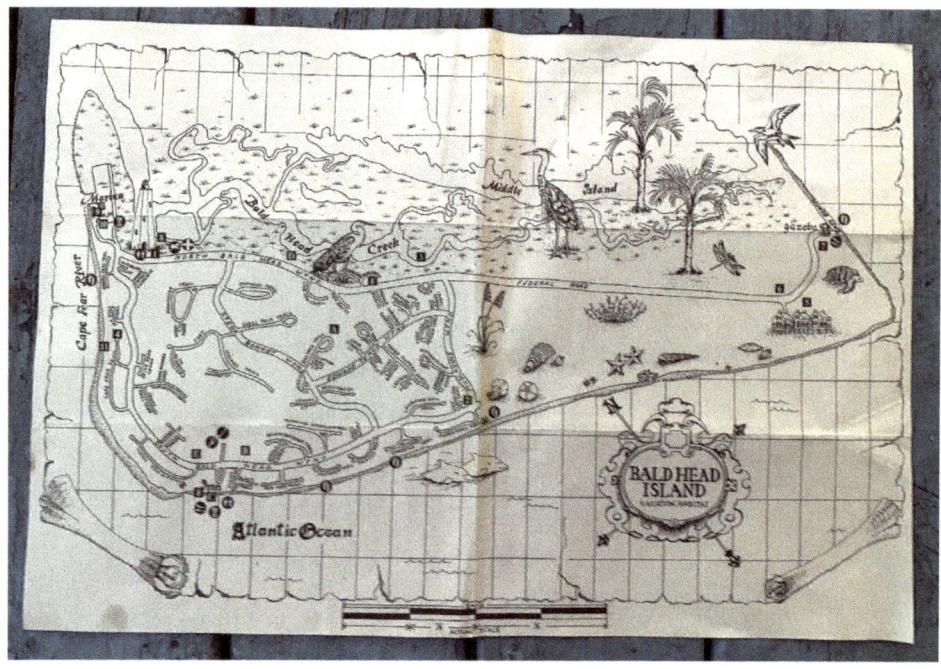

Bald Head Island map given to visitors in 1985. Photo courtesy of Harper Peterson.

departments, as well as two island caretakers, Spunky and Vicki Burton, who lived in a trailer by the lighthouse. "It was a small handful of people who helped to bring the island to new life," Harper says.

On the sales side, John Messick, Buck Timberlake, Brookie Sterling, and Draden Moore represented the core of the real estate team. Because each of them personally felt a strong attachment to the island, it was easy for them to sell it from that positive perspective. But that still required the right buyer who was willing to "rough it." At that time, the marina had only begun construction, electricity had literally just arrived, and there still wasn't a grocery store. "You simply wouldn't be here in that time and place if you didn't absolutely love Bald Head Island," Harper says.

To help with the marketing efforts, Christi Golden was hired fresh out of college to initially work as a copywriter; over time, she rose to become the island's marketing director. Initially, Christi and the marketing department believed their primary demographic was relocating retirees. In reality, they discovered about 90 percent of the residences on the island were second homes. For almost thirty years, there have consistently been only about 250 year-round residents on Bald Head Island, yet these residents have always been and remain the heart of the community. They work, volunteer, and truly hold BHI together.

Armed with this new information, the marketing team aimed to "emphasize the actual" when trying to promote the island. Christi describes this as trying to present the island truthfully, never attempting to sell BHI as something that it wasn't. They didn't want

Vicki Burton, caretaker and resident of Bald Head Island, and her daughter, Meris, in 1983. Photo courtesy of Melissa Burton.

to present it as if it were a luxurious five-star resort, because it simply wasn't. Bald Head Island was an authentic experience, more rooted in nature than artificiality, and so it was important for Christi and her team to communicate that.

Eventually a handful of dining options and other amenities became available and bigger and bigger houses were built, with many homeowners wanting luxuries such as subzero refrigerators, fancy stoves, and other high-end appliances. Donna Ray was happy to let the island's residents do as they pleased—but to her, Bald Head Island was meant to be a smaller, tight-knit, and rustic community. One with sandy wood floors, rusty old appliances, and a more rural, communal character. She wanted it to be practical and easygoing rather than frivolous and high-maintenance.

In the end, the people who stayed on the island were those who wanted to interact with all the different environments it offered, such as the creek, beaches, and forests. Hearkening back to the days of the Generator Society, people on Bald Head Island didn't come to be pampered but to experience nature.

Soon after Limited took control of Bald Head Island, Mark Mitchell invited Harper Peterson to open a bicycle rental station on the island. This weekend endeavor, combined with the newly established Island Passage outfitter store, was to promote more recreational pursuits on the island such as hiking, biking, sailing, and fishing. So, Harper brought four bicycles over from Wrightsville Beach and set up shop at the inn.

Plunkett Dodge, one of the newer residents on the island, managed Island Passage. She and Harper hit it off personally and professionally, and soon the two married and opened a little boutique together at the inn.

A few years later, they also opened Riverside Adventure Company, which offers resort wear, toys, and gifts. "I just follow her lead," Harper says. "Some of our ideas have failed, some have succeeded, but we've had fun doing it all. We've made some wonderful relationships and rich memories with our clients over the years."

Harper considers the island fortunate to have the Mitchells as developers, believing that they complemented the Generator Society's pioneering, free-spirited personalities. "I give thanks and credit to the whole Mitchell family, because if it wasn't for them we wouldn't be in [the] special place that it continues to be," he says.

Members of the Generator Society tend to have a different perspective. Many battles were waged between the "landowners" and the "developer" in town hall meetings and discussions, leading some to conclude that the Mitchells were only concerned about commercializing the island.

James Poole, one of the Generator Society members, saw both sides. "I don't think people understand how the Mitchells kept the island afloat," he explains. "It was not doing well for a long time. Yes, they took it over and wanted to glamorize the island but they didn't get to develop [all] they wanted. And that was because they were fighting the old guard who held its own and kept Bald Head Island what it is."

So, in essence, both Harper and James are correct: it took both groups to create and maintain the island as it is today.

Island Passage. Original artwork by Nancy Giacci.

PLAN

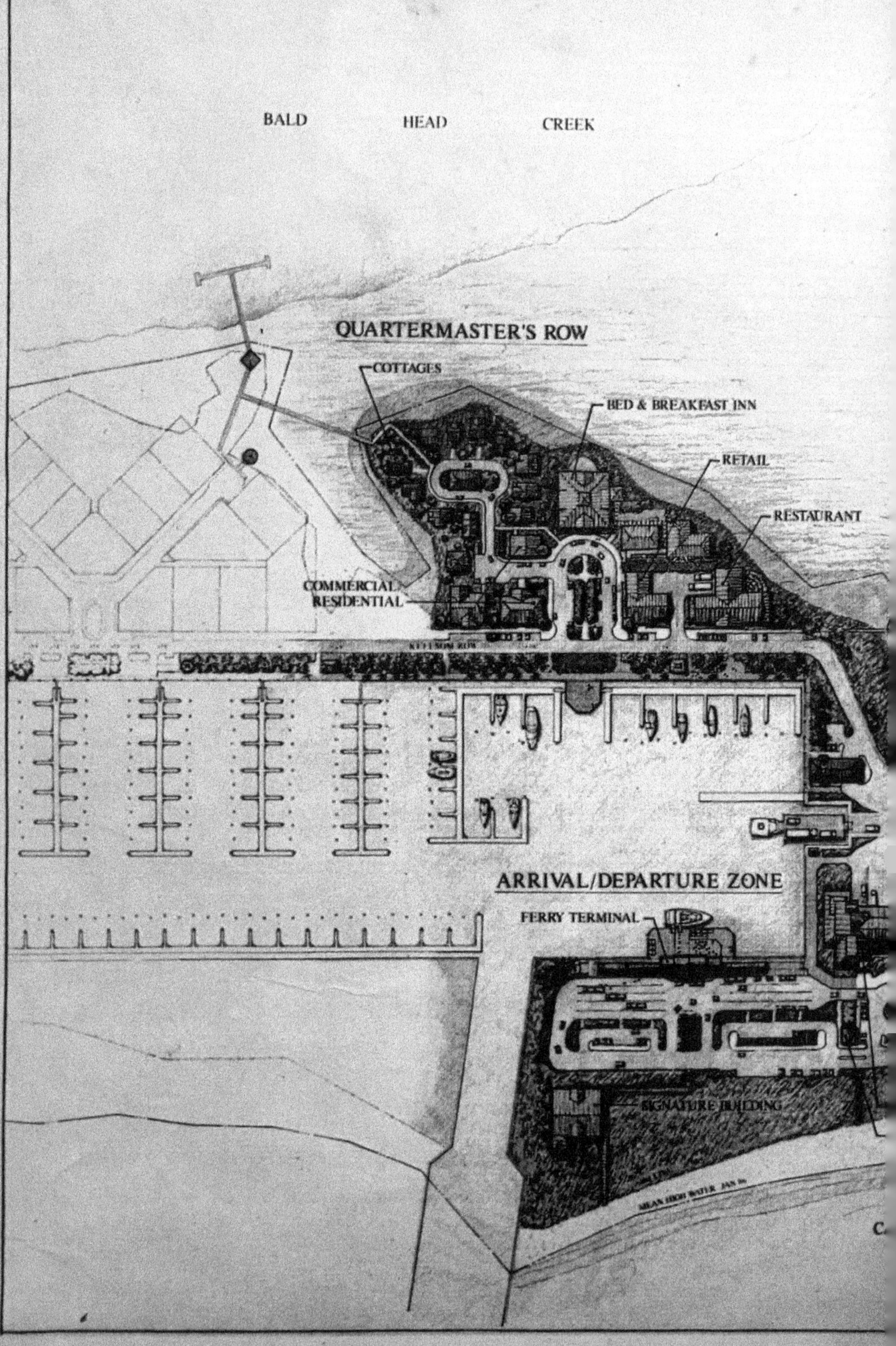

BALD HEAD CREEK

QUARTERMASTER'S ROW
- COTTAGES
- BED & BREAKFAST INN
- RETAIL
- RESTAURANT
- COMMERCIAL RESIDENTIAL

KEELSON RUN

ARRIVAL/DEPARTURE ZONE
- FERRY TERMINAL
- SIGNATURE BUILDING

MEAN HIGH WATER JAN 86

Chapter 30
Bald Head Association & the Village

In 1982, the Bald Head Island Property Owners Association (BHI POA) changed its name, becoming Bald Head Association (a.k.a. "BHA" and "Association").

Then in 1985, the Association worked to incorporate Bald Head Island as a municipality, citing concerns over nearby towns such as Southport wanting to annex the island into their own municipalities. This transition from a private island government to a public legal entity allowed for better planning and governance, and offered additional benefits—such as turning assessment fees into tax-deductible city taxes, providing greater law enforceability and fire protection, and selling alcoholic beverages at various locations on the island.

Pat Miller, whose husband, Ken, once served as Association president, recalls how every change on Bald Head Island caused contention . . . particularly when a second lane was added to Federal Road. "When they began cutting down trees, we pitched fits," Pat says. "The project actually stopped three times before it was ultimately completed. Of course, today we look back and think, *What would we do now if we didn't have two lanes on Federal Road?*"

Despite such tensions, she and her husband—and the majority of other property owners—refused to let politics drive them away from their beloved oasis.

Bald Head Island welcome sign with Old Baldy in the background. Early 1980s. Photo courtesy of Donna Ray.

Bald Head Island Post Office. Photo courtesy of Sharon Lightbourne.

Once the incorporation was complete, the Association separated into two entities: one to oversee island revenues and expenses (Village Council, a.k.a. "Village") and one to handle advocacy, covenants, and environmental protections (Association).

Together, the Association and the Village operated eight committees: Administration and Finance, Architectural Review, Beach Spoil and Dune Erosion, Island Works and Utilities, Long Range Planning, Natural Resources and Beautification, Recreation and Education, and Safety and Security. The Association and the Village also worked alongside Limited to resolve problems caused by the rapid growth they were experiencing.

As the decade drew to a close, it was apparent that the Association and the Village had accomplished much. However, Bald Head Association's 1989 Annual Report outlined several pressing matters that remained, including a water storage and distribution system, improved transportation on the island and across the Cape Fear River, a place to store emergency vehicles, and a dedicated Town Hall that would also house a post office.

Today, these needs have long been met … and both the Association and the Village continue to effectively serve the residents of Bald Head Island.

As Pat Miller concludes, "We're at a crossroads here and as we pass the baton on to the next generation, I hope they accept the island for what it is and want to contribute to it rather than take what they can get out of it. That in the future, our children and our grandchildren will continue to have access to the beauty and nature that drew us here so long ago."

PART IV: OUTFITTER YEARS (1980s)

"Now we have two boats and a marina. What a change!"
—Harriet Poole

The Big Event

Chapter 31
Power to the People

By the close of 1980, electric cables had been laid from Fort Caswell to Bald Head Island, splicing operations were scheduled, and hookups on both ends were underway. Distribution of electricity was expected to begin in the new year and conclude by summer.[20]

Then, on Saturday, January 24, 1981—after almost a decade of waiting—the switch was thrown. Bald Head Island finally gained access to electricity.

It was a momentous occasion to be sure, but individual homeowners still had to wait their turn as Carolina Power and Light Company (CP&L) distributed power to each lot in stages[21]... after they'd paid the utility easement fee of $2,800.

CP&L
Carolina Power & Light Company
P. O. Box 4107 • Wilmington, N. C. 28406

September 12, 1979

RUSSELL H. LEE
General Manager
Eastern Division

Mr. James Harrington, Jr.
Bald Head Island Corporation
P. O. Box 820
Cary, North Carolina 27511

Dear Mr. Harrington:

In accordance with the provisions of the attached letter of intent, Carolina Power & Light Company agrees to extend electric service to Stage I of the Bald Head Island Development. This agreement is contingent upon CP&L receiving the necessary permits required to extend such service and upon not encountering unforeseen difficulties which would make the extension of such service economically and engineeringly impractical. In case such unforeseen difficulties arise, CP&L would inform you of the circumstances along with the reasons and reopen negotiations in an effort to resolve the difficulties. Should such negotiations be unsuccessful, the attached letter of intent will terminate.

CP&L proposes to extend service from its 110/23 KV substation at Southport to a switching station located on Bald Head Island, and to extend underground service from that point to the building sites in Stage I of the development.

If you agree to the conditions set forth in this letter and the attachment hereto, please execute the attached letter and return to me.

We are happy that an agreement was reached.

Sincerely,

Russell H. Lee

RHL/tf
Attachment

Letter from the electric company to BHI Corporation in 1979 outlining the next steps in the process of bringing electricity to the island.

---

[20] Thad Wester, BHI POA president, letter to property owners, December 9, 1980, private collection.

[21] John Messick, vice president of Bald Head Island Corporation, letter to property owners, 1981, private collection.

Bald Head Island
Property Owners Association, Inc.

103 WEST 27TH STREET • LUMBERTON, NORTH CAROLINA 28358

January 6, 1981

Dear Property Owners:

     We now have firm commitment for the power hookup and celebration at Bald Head. The date and time is Saturday, January 24th at 2:00 p.m.

     All property owners are invited by Bald Head Island, Inc. to the "Energizing Party" (complete with champagne) to be held at Bald Head Inn. Please R.S.V.P. to either John Messick or myself so that appropriate transportation, etc. can be arranged. Please note that the Inn will not be open for overnight guests nor have food service. For those needing to return to the mainland afterwards, transportation will be arranged.

     This represents a major milestone in the history of Bald Head and, hopefully, many of you will be part of the celebration. We hope to see you then.

Sincerely,

BALD HEAD PROPERTY OWNERS ASSOCIATION, INC.

Thad B. Wester, M. D., President

TBW/mm

Invitation to property owners to attend the power hookup celebration.

The Tree House receives its electric meter box shortly before BHI receives electricity.

Thad Wester, president of the BHI POA, speaks to property owners in attendance at the power hookup celebration.

Thad and Lee Wester beam smiles as bright as the light bulb in front of them.

Once electricity from the Brunswick Nuclear Power Station began pulsing throughout the entire island, life became a bit easier—and quieter—for the pioneers. Without the drone of generators, silence enveloped BHI. Water flowed freely into houses without the need of hand pumps or leaky water tanks in the attic. No more stubbed toes as residents stumbled through a dark house after shutting off the generator for the night. Food could be kept cold in full-size refrigerators and—best of all—ice could be made every day, in every house.

But soon, many of the people who had eagerly awaited electricity for years found themselves missing the generator lifestyle. Despite all their quirks and challenges, the generators had become an integral part of their island lives.

Everyone was accustomed to electricity back home on the mainland; Bald Head Island had been the only place they could escape the modern trappings of city life. Yes, the generator lifestyle may have required much more physical work, but it also offered a greater sense of accomplishment. The ability to be creative and problem-solve, to rely on neighbors daily … it made them appreciate the little things in life.

Billy Dunlap was somewhat disappointed when they finally got electricity—because then he discovered he'd had a lot of fun living without it.

In the months and years following the flip of the switch, each of the Generator Society families would reflect on the past and agree with Leslie Thomas, who summarizes, "I wouldn't trade those days for anything."

Landmark Structures

Chapter 32
Bald Head Inn

It was with high hopes and big plans that Carolina Cape Fear Corporation constructed Bald Head Inn in 1972. Built in conjunction with the eighteen-hole championship golf course, they envisioned the two projects attracting wealthy weekend travelers and summer vacationers who, after experiencing the unique beauty of the island, would potentially become property owners.

Located on South Beach a couple hundred yards in front of where the Bald Head Club currently stands, the inn had welcomed many of the early pioneers—first when they received a tour of the island and then again as their homes were built. Even when families preferred to camp on their lots during their home construction phase, the inn still served as a welcome refuge.

There was the time, for example, when the Pooles were caught unaware by a driving rainstorm, which forced them to abandon their tents for safety at the inn. "We were greeted with open arms," Frank recalls. "The inn crew always treated us like kings."

Before their house was built, the Pooles spent many weekends camping at BHI. Photo courtesy of Harriet and Cindy Poole.

The inn hosted many new prospects as well, but the failing economy continued to reduce the number of BHI visitors every year. Slowly, as CCFC began applying every dollar earned toward their debts, the inn began to experience the perils of neglect. When adequate overnight lodging could no longer be offered, the inn continued to operate as a restaurant only. But by the time CCFC went into foreclosure in 1975, the inn was completely abandoned.

It was during this time that Harriet Poole recalls using the inn's kitchen to prepare food for Generator Society parties. "I can still see Frank washing oysters at the big stainless steel sink for everyone," she says. "During those years when no one managed it, we'd all use it."

When Bald Head Island Corporation took over, it seems they revived the inn since it was included in a 1978 BHI POA survey of its members. The survey questions related to the property owners' future expectations for the island, their recent experiences while visiting the island, and their satisfaction levels with the developer, the Association, and the services (such as the inn and transportation).

The anonymous responses ranged from complimentary to critical, yet together offer a candid snapshot of what the inn was like at that time:

- "Very good considering the circumstances."
- "Only real problem is incertainty [sic] of electric power."
- "We enjoyed everything including temporary inconvenience (failure of generator)."
- "Food service good but limited."
- "Service fine—problem—no hot water."
- "Okay when generator is working."
- "No hot water, no air conditioning, no drapes at window."
- "A bit rustic (no hot water!)."
- "Air conditioning was not working. No screens on doors. Need I say more?"

In 1980, the recently restructured Bald Head Island Corporation remodeled the inn, adding new boardwalks, lagoons, and the island's first telephone—a pay phone. Nevertheless, Doug Anderson recalls how they continued to communicate by CB radio even in the early '80s. "One time we were sitting at the inn talking to someone on the mainland and all of a sudden, the connection went absolutely, totally dead. So we were sitting there with a CB radio in our hand with nobody to talk to."

That was a common experience.

Keith Bradley, who vacationed on Bald Head Island for years before purchasing a villa in 1994, remembers that quirk and explains: "Early on—pre-cell phones—you had to watch for ship traffic on the river since a vessel could block the microwave signal to the mainland."

Bald Head Island Inn. Original artwork by Nancy Giacci.

A view of the inn from across the dunes. Original artwork by Nancy Giacci.

The Bald Head Island Inn as the tide comes in. Original artwork by Nancy Giacci.

A marketing letter dated August 22, 1980 promotes the restored inn as now offering "eight comfortable beachfront rooms—each with a balcony overlooking the Atlantic. Dining facilities are excellent and [are] highlighted each evening with a cocktail party followed by a candlelight dinner."

```
              BALD HEAD ISLAND INN
                  1982 SEASON
         EUROPEAN PLAN - DOUBLE OCCUPANCY

         DAILY RATE              $ 70.00
         Friday, Saturday

         DAILY RATE              $ 65.00
         Sunday-Thursday

         WEEKLY RATE             $450.00
         Seven nights

 ADD $10.00 per day for each additional person.  Children under twelve
   (12) - no additional charge.  Maximum occupancy - Four (4)
                     DINING ROOM OPEN
                   8:00 A.M. - 9:00 P.M.
                        INN OPEN
         Friday Through Sunday noon in March and April
        Seven days per week from May thru September 17th
       Fridays & Saturdays in September, October & November
                   Open Thanksgiving Week
           Other dates available for groups upon request
                   CHECK OUT TIME 12 NOON
                    CHECK IN TIME  2 P.M.
 ROUNDTRIP TRANSPORTATION FROM SOUTHPORT TO ISLAND $5.00 PER PERSON
                    FOR RESERVATIONS WRITE:
                     Bald Head Island Corporation
                          P.O. Box 11058
                        Southport, NC  28461
                            OR CALL:
                         (919) 457-6763
```

Bald Head Inn amenities and rates for the 1982 season. Photo courtesy of Harriet and Cindy Poole.

The design of the inn was as unique as the island itself. Whereas typical hotels contain all their rooms in one building, the Bald Head Inn featured a cluster of small octagonal buildings connected by boardwalks. One of the buildings contained the front desk, kitchen, dining room, and bar. Each of the remaining four buildings contained two guest rooms with private baths.

Doug Anderson describes the inn complex as being "on stilts, an octagonal pod-type thing [with] a bar out beyond the restaurant; it was a lovely place to eat." Keith Bradly agrees that the inn offered great cuisine, claiming the New York cheesecake was "to die for." Indeed, the inn quickly became known for its excellent food service, becoming a sought-after venue for weddings and special events. Bo and Mildred Caperton, for example, celebrated their twenty-fifth wedding anniversary there.

"The only place to go out on the island in the early '80s was the inn so you got to know everyone pretty quickly," says Harper Peterson. Charlotte Dunlap adds, "The inn was the place to gather; it was the social scene of the island."

The Bald Head Island Inn dining room in 1983. The ocean and Villas are seen from the windows. Photo courtesy of Carol and Draden Moore.

It was also the most exciting place to be during high tide. "Ocean waves would sweep beneath the floorboards," Donna Ray recalls. "The waves would roll beneath your feet as you were having dinner." Similarly, Ann Cathcart remembers her kids sitting on the balcony railing outside their guest room and the ocean splashing up over their dangling legs. This novelty, however, would ultimately become the inn's demise.

The relentless tides and occasional strong storms eventually eroded the building's foundation to the point that, in May 1989, the inn was bulldozed and its pieces hauled away. "If the inn were still standing today," says Donna, "it would be hundreds of meters out into the ocean."

The Bald Head Island Inn in 1986. Photo courtesy of Nancy Giacci.

Beachfront views of the inn's room balconies during low tide.

Waves crashing against the foundation of the Bald Head Inn. Photo courtesy of Melinda Freeman.

Sandbags attempt to protect Bald Head Inn. Photo courtesy of BHI Association's Bald Head Island newsletter, summer 1983. Photographer: Kelly Carlton.

The sandbags are dry now, but when high tide comes, the ocean will lap at the foundation of the Bald Head Inn. The island corporation will move the luxurious, eight-room hotel back about 200 feet after April 1, putting it closer to the lobby and dining room complex and farther away from the waves.

Bald Head Inn Cheeseballs

1 pound cream cheese

1 pound grated sharp cheddar cheese

8 ounces (approx.) bleu cheese dressing (Roka or equal)

1 teaspoon Worcestershire sauce

½ teaspoon garlic salt

1 dash salt

chopped nuts (pecans or walnuts)

maraschino cherries

In a large bowl, mix cream cheese, grated cheddar, and bleu cheese dressing together. Then add all other ingredients. Mix well. Allow to stand 6–8 hours in refrigerator or until chilled. Once well chilled, make into 3 similarly sized balls. Roll in chopped nuts. Garnish with candied cherries. Keeps well in the freezer.

Caviar Pie

6 hard-boiled eggs, chopped

3 Tablespoons mayonnaise

1 cup red onion, minced fine

8 ounces cream cheese, softened

2/3 cup sour cream

black caviar

lemon, sliced into wedges

sprigs of parsley

Mix the eggs with the mayonnaise. Spread on bottom of oiled 8-inch spring pan or pie pan. Sprinkle with the minced onion and set aside. Blend the cream cheese with the sour cream until smooth. Spread over minced onion with wet spatula. Chill for 3 hours.

To serve:
Spread and cover top with black caviar. Knife around the sides of pan. Lift off the spring belt or cut into wedges and lift out with a pie knife and arrange on a serving platter. Garnish with lemon wedges and parsley. Serve with good crackers. Makes 10–12 servings.

Berne Jambalaya

The first Smith Island Social was organized by the Bernes and Westers, who cooked jambalaya together at the inn for everyone.

¼ cup oil

2 cups cooked diced chicken

1 pound sausage (andouille)

1 pound peeled raw shrimp

4 cups chopped onions

2 cups chopped celery

2 cups chopped green pepper

1 tablespoon chopped garlic

4 cups cooked rice

2 cups canned tomatoes

2 teaspoons salt (heaping)

2 cups chopped green onions

cayenne pepper to taste

Cook sausage. Remove from pot. Sauté onions, celery, green pepper, and garlic to the tenderness that you desire. Add canned tomatoes and other seasonings. Add chicken and sausage. You may need to add a little chicken broth if too thick. Let simmer. Just before serving, add shrimp and simmer for about 5 minutes. Add cooked rice and heat through.

Chapter 33
Old Baldy Lighthouse

The first lighthouse on the island was constructed in 1794. But less than twenty years later, it was torn down due to the ever-approaching proximity of the ocean. The second lighthouse—Old Baldy, the stucco one everyone is familiar with today—was built in 1817 on a bluff. Throughout the nineteenth and early twentieth centuries, Old Baldy alerted ships to their proximity to the island and the swift currents of the Cape Fear River.

By the early 1980s, the lighthouse was in a severe state of disrepair stemming primarily from rain damage. Donna Ray took it upon herself to spearhead the effort to restore it. After applying for and receiving nonprofit status by the government, the Old Baldy Foundation was born in 1985, with Donna initially serving as president and Jane Oakley as executive director. Approximately seventy island families made significant financial contributions to their "Steps to the Top" fundraiser.

Old Baldy Lighthouse. Photo courtesy of Harriet and Cindy Poole.

With an initial $25,000 grant the foundation commissioned an engineering study to examine the extent of the damages and provide a listing of all the necessary repairs. Once the report came back, Donna and her team got to work, using the donated funds to tackle one repair at a time. Of course, that's how everything got done on Bald Head Island: through hard work, one step at a time, with the help of a strong and dedicated community.

Although no longer operational (it was deactivated in 1935), "Old Baldy" remains North Carolina's oldest standing lighthouse and is the main attraction on the island, as it continues to offer spectacular views to those willing to make the winding-staircase ascent.

Chapter 34
Village Chapel

The Chapel holds a special place in the hearts of many Bald Head Island property owners. It was conceived by Harriet Poole and Lee Wester, who initially scheduled an Easter Sunday service at the inn. "The services were held in the bar quad, with the alcohol covered," recalls Keith Bradley.

"We tried to make the bar look as much like a church as possible," explains Harper Peterson. "John Messick and I got bedsheets and threw them over the liquor bottles and that was the pulpit."

Next they had to locate a minister. "I went to the Seamen's Center at the State Port in Wilmington and met Jan Smook, a Presbyterian minister from South Africa who had immigrated here with his wife, Sylvia," Harper says. "Jan was a delightful man; tall with a big beard. He agreed to give the sermon."

An estimated forty people turned out for that inaugural service in 1984. When subsequent Sunday morning attendance quickly exceeded capacity, it became apparent that a dedicated chapel was needed to meet the non-denominational worshipers' needs. But where should it be built? A chapel committee was created and discussions ensued, but with another Easter fast approaching, a temporary venue was required immediately. The grounds of the Old Baldy Lighthouse was selected.

"Easter sunrise service was kind of a pivotal point for the island," Harper says. "The Mitchells and their whole extended family came to the island for that Easter service of 1985. The no-see-ums arrived as well, but they didn't deter anybody. Jan spoke from the doorway of the lighthouse at sunrise; it was just spectacular. And then many of us went to the inn afterward; it was packed with people as well."

It was such a meaningful event that the Easter service at Old Baldy became an annual tradition. "Dr. Jan Smook always came to Bald Head Island to give the sunrise service sermon," says Harriet Poole. "He looked like an apostle from the Bible [as he] stood in the doorway of the lighthouse with the grounds … filled with people. Dr. Smook always spent the night before at our house. Frank would then take him down to the lighthouse while Carolyn Fleming and I fixed coffee and so forth for everyone to have after the service."

Cindy Poole recalls how her mother helped "pass the plate" at the services and one time looked up into the face of Willard Scott, best known as the *Today* show's weather reporter for many years.

Donna Ray attended the Island's annual Easter services and remembers how the morning sun's radiant glow would rise over waters far off in the horizon, just as the Island's residents gathered together. "Every year, one man would sing at the bottom of the lighthouse," she recalls. "His voice reverberated throughout the tower as its acoustics carried the notes through the morning air. It never failed to send a chill down your spine—like the music of a dream."

The Rev. Jan Smook, in the lighthouse doorway, conducted the Bald Head Easter sunrise service for the ninth consecutive time Sunday.

Easter sunrise services continued to draw large crowds into the next decade, as evidenced by this newspaper clipping from the April 22, 1992 issue of *The State Port Pilot*.

Dr. Jan Smook (left) conducted the baptism of Plunkett Dodge (middle) and Harper Peterson's (right) son, Will, at the chapel in 1990.

Inside of the chapel. Photo courtesy of Hank Schmulling.

According to Harper Peterson, George and Cynthia Mitchell were so impressed by the 1985 Easter sunrise service that they donated the land adjacent to the lighthouse for the construction of the chapel and even commissioned an architect—Clovis Heimsath of Texas. A groundbreaking ceremony followed the 1986 Easter service, with construction of the chapel funded entirely through property owner donations. "Many of the brass medallions placed along the altar rail are inscribed with the names of these important early donors," Harper says.

The chapel's traditional cruciform floor plan seats up to 120 persons and offers worshipers a tranquil view of Bald Head Creek, Middle Island, and Bluff Island through a series of large windows behind the altar. Natural light filters through two original stained glass windows designed by Marianne Heimsath. The first, at the rear of the nave, features a tripartite fish design depicting the Holy Trinity (three in one) and is a memorial to Buck Timberlake. The second features a dove with twelve golden rays around it, representing Jesus and the twelve apostles. Located above the organ, this window is dedicated to the memory of John Messick.

Although construction wasn't 100 percent complete, it was dedicated after the 1987 Easter sunrise service, and soon guest ministers were invited to provide weekly Sunday sermons and stay with committee members at their island homes. Hosting the ministers became a popular tradition that lasted two years before a small apartment was constructed next to the chapel for their accommodations.

Also on the grounds of the chapel, just inside the fence and invisible to most people, is a metal pole enveloped by an oak tree. Keith Bradley explains that the pole at one time supported a CB antenna that was the only means of communication for one of the early island caretakers that predated the Generator Society.

The Chapel's steeple placement. Photo courtesy of Donna Ray.

Bald Head Island Chapel under construction. Photos courtesy of Hank Schmulling.

Ann Cathcart was always amazed and appreciative of the ingenuity and resilience of the people of Bald Head Island. "We just always try to figure out how to make things work," she says.

For example, she often helped greet and seat worshipers on Sunday mornings for the two morning services. She recalls one particular summer Sunday when the minister collapsed during his first sermon due to dehydration and was taken to Southport for medical attention. With another service scheduled for ten o'clock but no minister, Ann assumed it would be canceled. But to her surprise, the guest violinist stepped up and said, "My dad's a minister and is on the ferry, coming to listen to me play at ten o'clock. I bet he'd preach."

So Ann and a few others ran to the ferry, met the man at the boat, and said, "Excuse me. We don't have a minister; do you think you could preach? You're on in twenty minutes." He accepted and did such a great job that he was invited back as a visiting minister several times. "He turned out to be an absolutely delightful person and a great preacher. We always think we're in charge, but that just proves God is," Ann says.

Jim Brown, another of the chapel's regular rotating ministers, received many requests to officiate various ceremonies. "I've done lots of weddings and memorial services, some baby dedications, and of course a lot of sermons," he says. In addition to officiating at the chapel, he has also been asked to lead ceremonies at other locations on the island as well. "Six weddings were at the top of the lighthouse and four were at sunrise, one was on the ferry heading toward the island, and many on the beach and at the clubs," he recalls.

Bald Head Island Chapel. Original artwork by Nancy Giacci.

Harper Peterson and Plunkett Dodge were the first couple to be married in the chapel; Amanda Wester and her fiancé were the second. "Henry proposed in September on the chapel deck overlooking the marsh," Amanda says. "We then went to the marina where they helped us make all our calls to the family [via CB] since there were no phones. After the wedding ceremony at the chapel, the inn prepared our food for the wedding breakfast and served beer and wine. I remember Dad couldn't believe beer was a dollar a can! He later said, 'Your friends drank a lot of beer,' but would never tell us how much. Our wedding breakfast was the last function at the inn before it was demolished."

Vicki Young has also celebrated numerous life events at the chapel. "Two of my children had their weddings on the island and five of the grandchildren were christened in the chapel." And two of James Poole's three boys got married there. "It was very special," he says.

Bald Head Island's chapel has meant a lot of things to a lot of people over the years. "From my first entering the chapel I was drawn to the beauty and sanctity of this holy place," says Keith Bradley. "Looking across the marsh, it reveres God's creation and truly is a place of worship."

Yet perhaps no one can describe the chapel's impact on their lives as eloquently as Pat Miller, who considers the chapel the "heart" of the island:

View of Old Baldy Lighthouse from the chapel's window.
Photo courtesy of Patricia and Charlie Young.

"Personally, some of the most important events in my life have taken place at the chapel. I have introduced my children to a broader meaning of faith, celebrated anniversaries, watched the marriage of my child, and buried my husband within these walls. I have found a healing place to meditate, a beautiful location to rejoice [in], and a peaceful place to grieve. I have grown in knowledge, made new friends, been exposed to an array of outstanding ministers from a variety of denominations, and experienced beautiful music that fills the wooden rafters. When my final breath is taken, I will be scattered on the grounds to remain part of the Circle of Life on Bald Head Island. What a privilege it has been to have been allowed the opportunity to proclaim the Good News on this special island. I have been blessed beyond my wildest expectations by my involvement with the chapel and, looking towards the legacy I hope to leave behind, my wish is to continue offering this experience to future generations."

Just as the chapel is a treasured place to celebrate life, its grounds also offers a peaceful place to honor and remember those who have passed on. The property features a scatter garden created in honor of Bo and Mildred Caperton, who loved Bald Head Island so much they wanted their ashes to remain there. This sacred and revered plot of ground contains not only their ashes but those of many other former Bald Head Island property owners as well, each of them remembered with small markers bearing their names.

Several live oak trees have also been dedicated to a handful of former residents who made significant contributions to the services and preservation of Bald Head Island. Located throughout the island, these trees represent the strength and beauty that arose from ideas planted long ago, carefully nurtured and pruned through the turbulent growth stages. The trees and the people they represent remain part of the past, present, and future of Bald Head Island.

Outfitter Experiences

Chapter 35
Official Outfitters

"Outfitters" were the summer concierges of Bald Head Island. Familiar with the lifestyle, lore, and locations of BHI, they welcomed prospective buyers, shuttled people and luggage, and generally capitalized on the knowledge and experiences they had acquired while living part-time on the island.

Leslie Thomas worked as an outfitter for two summers when she was in high school, doing whatever was needed. On many hot summer days, that included getting visitors more "island diamonds," more commonly known as ice.

Marshall Dunlap lived and worked on Bald Head Island as an outfitter during his ninth-grade summer vacation, circa 1985. In that capacity he did everything from giving island tours to washing dishes at the inn. Most of the time, however, he picked people up when they arrived at the creek-side dock before the marina was built. It was an incredible summer job for a fifteen-year-old.

It didn't matter that he was too young for a driver's license; the year prior, the island had banned traditional vehicles, replacing them with golf carts. So, to Marshall, it was thrilling to be able to drive golf carts around all day—especially the time he shuttled his hero Dean Smith, the legendary UNC basketball coach, to one of the villas.

Guests being driven to their destination in one of the island's multi-passenger golf cart "trams." Courtesy of Bald Head Island newsletter, BHI Association, 1982.

At the time, there were only about thirty-five houses on the island. Each house had a name, and Marshall knew them all by heart. If someone asked to be taken to Sunset House or Beach Haven, Marshall knew exactly where to drive them. The tipping point for him was when the island transitioned from a recognizable number of individual houses to a sprawling collection of hundreds of houses. It was a melancholy sort of feeling to not know everyone anymore. The population curve had exploded.

Kellie Terrell (Bo and Mildred Caperton's granddaughter) returned to the island in 1983 after living abroad for a few years and was shocked at the paved roads, electricity, and additional houses. Yet it was still a wonderful place to explore, since she lived on Bald Head Island with her grandparents for a couple of summers. She recalls dragging shrimp nets through the marina with the Wester kids when it was shallow while under construction. "We ate some great shrimp," she says. With the development of the marina came the first convenience store, "which was a thrill," James Poole says. "It was a little small gas station with staple items."

From the Bald Head Lighthouse construction work at the island marina appears to be at a standstill. Despite the impression, work has been progressing on schedule, and with the recent delivery of a new dredge, about five acres, or half, of the marina is expected to be dredged by late June. Other Phase 1 work expected to be completed by that time is the construction of a permanent facility for the island's passenger boat and about twelve finger piers for the island's boat owners.

Bald Head Island Marina under construction. Photo courtesy of BHI Association's Bald Head Island newsletter, summer 1983. Photographer: Kelly Carlton.

View of the marina from Old Baldy Lighthouse. Photo courtesy of Carol and Draden Moore.

Thad Wester speaking at the marina opening celebration. Photo courtesy of Carol and Draden Moore.

Kellie also held several jobs during that time, one of which was working for Tom Plankers at the pro shop. Only after she was hired did she realize that his assistant, Homer, was the man who used to fuss at her and her cousin Jeff for finding abandoned golf carts and driving them twenty or thirty feet until the batteries died again.

Primarily, though, Kellie worked as an outfitter in the early days when luggage was transferred off the boat one piece at a time, hand-over-hand from boat to dock. (Only a few things ended up in the water.) Her duties included driving the island guests to their homes on the tram and carrying luggage up the steps to their houses, calling "outfitter mobile to the *Adventure*" on the VHF (Very High Frequency) marine radio many times a day, and getting to ride on the top deck of the *Adventure* over to Southport and back in the late evenings. "Being on the water on the boat at night was so fun," she says.

The second ferry, *Revenge*, sits docked at the marina in front of the new Chandler building, which housed the dock master, a small convenience store, and various administration offices (including the real estate office). Photo courtesy of Harriet and Cindy Poole

Occasionally she gave the dinner package tour, which provided visitors with a meal at the inn followed by a scenic tour of the island. And sometimes she aided stragglers who had missed the last passenger ferry of the day, taking them along with inn employees to the marina to catch a ride home in the crew boat. "The drive there with the people was always fun but the drive back without them could be a little dark and lonely," she reflects. "Sometimes I went home via the beach road (South Bald Head Wynd), but when I was feeling extra brave, I drove down North Bald Head Wynd and Stede Bonnet until I came out on South Bald Head Wynd."

Kellie's sister Shelley, although never an outfitter, stayed equally busy with a variety of part-time jobs. These included babysitting, helping at day camps, working at a dress shop, assisting the tennis pro, and pedaling the first ice cream cart around the island.

Stede Bonnet was beautiful and inviting during the day but eerie and intimidating at night. Courtesy of Harriet and Cindy Poole.

Pat Miller's son Matt made money for college by driving the tram. It was a fairly mundane job, transporting loads of people from the ferry to their houses for a week on the island. Except the time a girl ran toward him screaming, "My friend is drowning in the ocean!" Matt knew about the island's strong rip currents, so he quickly parked the tram before jumping into the ocean and swimming out to the struggling girl. Worried that her flailing arms would pull him under and cause them both to drown, he waited until she was exhausted before grabbing her and pulling her ashore.

He came home dripping wet. Pat took one look at him and asked, "Did you run into a rainstorm on the island?" When he told her he'd just saved somebody's life, she didn't believe him … until the entire community started talking about it.

"The Bald Head Island police chief nominated him for the North Carolina Community Hero Award, which he received," Pat recalls. "It made me very proud of my son and it's meant a lot to our family."

Chapter 36
Sanctuary

During their first visit to Bald Head Island in 1981, Ann Cathcart and her family ate dinner at the inn, which she described as being "so cool." The entire island captured their imagination on that trip, leading them to continue coming as often as they could.

Her conclusion, after years of hosting guests on the island, was that a person either really loves Bald Head Island or really hates it. The Cathcarts immediately fell in love with it and ultimately bought a villa, which would become their special place. "We named our villa Sanctuary because that's exactly what it is to us: a sanctuary," Ann says.

In the early '80s, property owners made their own fun. Whether the kids wanted to or not, families spent time together. Thus, the Cathcarts played board games and walked on the beach. Sometimes they found the bioluminescence in the sand. At night they gathered on the deck while a neighbor, Dr. Ben Gasque from Lumberton, set up his telescope and taught them about the constellations. "It was so dark back then," Ann remembers, "we could just stretch out on our backs on the deck, look up, and see all the stars."

Sunday afternoons often found them biking around the island to look at whatever new house was being built. Everyone had "the key to the island" since builders didn't lock up the houses back then, allowing residents to go in and critique the designs. "You can't do that anymore," she says, "but it was great fun."

After Ann's husband passed away, she chose to move to Bald Head Island in order to grieve among the community she loved so much. "My friends in Raleigh were wonderfully supportive and so good to me and I loved them," she explains, "but down at Bald Head Island, it just was easier and more comforting."

In Raleigh, for example, it wasn't customary for people to walk along the road to chat with neighbors, and they certainly weren't likely to just show up unannounced at your door.

At Bald Head Island, however, people were always stopping by her villa. "Community is the essence of the island to me," she says. "Bald Head Island just has it, and it's easy to become a part of it. It's not forced; it's comforting. It offers a pleasant, different way of life."

Chapter 37
The Hobbit Hole

When Harper Peterson's father, Harold Peterson, retired from Grumman Aircraft in 1985, he relocated to Bald Head Island and became a member of Harper's retail team. "He was so involved and instrumental to the character and culture of the island that people often think he was a founder," Harper says. "He added that special spirit." He became so well liked that soon everyone was affectionately calling him "Pops."

Part of his job was to maintain and repair the rented golf carts, bicycles, and other equipment that the steady stream of visitors used. Whereas most people would build a repair shop to do such work, Pops dug out what became known at the "Hobbit Hole" underneath the old Riverside store, which was located around the corner from where it currently stands.

"You had to duck down to get in there," Harper recalls, "but once inside he had his coffee pot, his radio, a couple of chairs . . . it quickly became a gentleman's club." It was not uncommon to find five or six men there, simply hanging out and talking. Willard Scott, the weatherman on the *Today* show, owned a home on Bald Head Island and was one of his frequent visitors. "He and my dad were good friends, like everyone was back then," Harper says.

One morning in 1989, Harper got a call from a BHI resident notifying him that Willard Scott had just talked about his dad on national television. While giving the weather report for the East Coast, Willard trailed off and said something to the effect of, "I wonder what Pops is doing right now? It must be beautiful on Bald Head."

Harold "Pops" Peterson in the Hobbit Hole under Island Passage where he served coffee and cake to his customers. Courtesy of Harper Peterson.

Television personalities weren't the only notable people Pops befriended. When Mike and Mary Easley—the future governor and first lady of North Carolina—started coming to the island, Pops helped them learn how to sail. So when Pops retired from his duties at Bald Head Island, he reached out to Mike to ask if he could find him some work. "Mike got him a job on the Fort Fisher Ferry," Harper says. "He worked until he was 98 years old as a deck hand; he's now 104 years old and active as ever with a sharp mind, still driving all over town with his dog, Bogart."

Chapter 38
Pure Madness … and Magic

Plunkett Dodge moved to Bald Head Island from Boston in 1984 with a baby and a three-year-old in order to work from home as an illustrator and do some wholesale work for the fashion industry. But moving from a large city to an island with only eighteen residents was a big adjustment.

No one had lived at *Captain Charlie's 1* for twenty years, but, since it had been promoted as a move-in-ready rental, Plunkett happily signed the lease. "The day I got there, I opened a closet and discovered a nest of snakes," she recalls. "No one told me the water wasn't potable, so all night long Addie and Alex were up vomiting from the juice I had mixed with the water. And throughout the night, I heard the sound of crushing bones as our cat found all kinds of things to eat." Without a single neighbor around to ask for help, Plunkett quickly discovered that you had to be independent to live on the island back then, but she was "totally game" for the adventure.

Although they had electricity, they didn't have air conditioning or central heat. So, since they arrived in the sweltering dog days of August, Plunkett relied on cool ocean breezes and minimal clothing to keep them from overheating. By January, however, when ocean breezes turned frigid, they warmed themselves around a newly installed wood stove.

"The beginning was pure madness," Plunkett says, "but it was also pure magic. It was there that my daughter, Addie, took her first steps and where we celebrated her first birthday. *Captain Charlie's* is permanently planted in my heart."

Plunkett Dodge in front of *Captain Charlie's Station* in 1985. Courtesy of Harper Peterson.

Captain Charlie's, that collection of little blue cottages at the north end of Bald Head Island, represented hope and beauty for Jerry Blow in early October 1985.

"The afternoon sun was glorious that day as Leigh and I stood on the front porch of *Capt. Charlie's* with the preacher," he reflects. "A couple dozen of our friends were on the dune at the bottom of the porch steps as a slight breeze blew from the south. It was almost magical. We all have some extra-special experiences in our lives; our wedding day on Bald Head Island was certainly one of mine!"

Jerry and Leigh's wedding at *Captain Charlie's* in 1985. Courtesy of Jerry Blow.

Chapter 39
Poncho & Fainting Joe Hill

Like an old pirate captain on the high seas, the late Joe Lee was rarely ever seen without a parrot on his shoulder. The vibrantly colored bird's name was Poncho, and he was as good a friend as he was a conversationalist. Whenever Joe went golfing, Poncho would ride shotgun in the golf cart, perched upon his shoulder until they reached the driving green. When they made it to the course, Joe would leave Poncho set up on the first hole to chat with the other golfers as they made their first swings off the tee.

Joe Lee and his parrot, Poncho, in the 1980s. Photo courtesy of Joey and Heather Lee.

Joe Lee's parrot, Poncho. Courtesy of Melinda Freeman.

Some bird owners have trouble trusting their pets, often locking them up in cramped cages all day for fear of them flying away. Joe Lee never had such problems because, truthfully, it'd be wrong to say that Joe owned Poncho. He let him sleep outside at night, and rarely ever put him in a cage. If he really wanted to, Poncho could have flown away at any moment, but he never did. For fifteen years, he stayed loyal to Joe, and Joe stayed loyal to him. Joe even went so far as to build a large swing on his porch for his companion to enjoy. The two of them shared a bond that most people couldn't have with another human, let alone an animal. It was a bond that lasted until the very end, when Poncho was snagged by a raccoon in the night. As tragic as that was, nobody could question that Poncho had lived a rich and storied life.

At one point, Joe Lee decided to get in shape. But, like all his other endeavors, his methods were less than conventional. After all, this is the same man who routinely played golf without shoes, so what Joe did next should come as no surprise. In his quest for fitness, he stuffed his golf bag with bricks and went down to the green. He planned to walk the entire length of the eighteen-hole golf course while carrying his brick-laden bag to build up his strength. And to Joe's credit, he managed to get through the first ten holes before suddenly collapsing from exhaustion on the fairway. To commemorate this, the golf course built a plaque on that very same hole in his honor, dubbing it "Fainting Joe Hill." The plaque lasted an entire decade before it was taken down.

Joe was never scared of life—he lived his to the fullest, and embraced all it had to offer. One time, he and his friend John Byrne decided to swim across the inlet to Fort Fisher. Today, the Fort is connected to the Island thanks to a hurricane that blew sand in from the north. But back then, they were completely separated by water.

During their swim, the pair realized the tides were far worse than what they had anticipated. The currents were fast and violent. For a time, neither one of them thought they would survive. But as they fought their way through the water, they managed to swim past the deadly current and make it back to shore. The two survived the encounter unscathed, but the experience left them with an unforgettable reminder of how powerful the ocean can truly be.

Another time, Joe was golfing on the eighteenth hole on a scorching summer afternoon. To beat the heat, he simply put down his club and jumped into a nearby lagoon. Seeing this, the course's pro raced over and pleaded with him to get out of the water because alligators were known to live there. It didn't faze Joe one bit. "Alligators are more scared of me than I am of them. Ain't gonna mess with me," he said as he continued his swim.

Joe loved the island and its people. He owned a jewelry store and always prepared little prewrapped gifts, "just in case." When he heard that someone in the community was having a rough time, or if a family member had recently passed away, he would show up at their house with one of his gifts to cheer them up. He was truly a generous soul, and he meant a great deal to everyone in the community.

Chapter 40
Legends, Nobles & Scalawags

Bald Head Island has had its fair share of legends, one of the most popular being Captain Charlie and the "Yayhoe" monster. Captain Charlie was the old Cape Fear Lighthouse keeper, and he told his children tales of the large but elusive monster as a warning to keep them from getting lost in the woods at night. According to Captain Charlie, the Yayhoe lurked in the forests and had a sharp, twisted horn where its head should have been.

It was a tradition that carried on long after the Captain's time, with Marshall Dunlap's parents using the Yayhoe as a way to keep him and the other kids close to the house. Marshall and his friends were certain that the Yayhoe lived at *Captain Charlie's Station*. After all, the three cottages were old, boarded up, and *looked* downright haunted.

When Marshall was an adult, he kept the tradition alive by telling Yayhoe stories to his children and their friends as well, even driving them around the island on golf carts to go on Yayhoe hunts. Most of the kids loved it, but a few were terrified.

Plunkett Dodge, who lived at *Captain Charlie's* for a time, never saw the Yayhoe. Her son Alex, however, encountered "Clodin" when he was three-and-a-half years old. Assuming Clodin was an imaginary friend, Plunkett played along and asked Alex how they met and what she looked like. When he proceeded to say that he met her on the landing of their stairwell and described her as having orange hair and wearing clothes that covered her hands, Plunkett's hair on the back of her neck stood up.

"I, too, had the feeling that there was a presence there, especially in *Captain Charlie's* #3," Plunkett says. "I often found myself turning around, looking for what I felt was there. Clodin's presence wasn't scary or mean; I think she really is there and she's sad. Several people have felt her ghost there. One person was lying in bed and felt someone lay down beside them."

Clodin is rumored to have been aboard a ship from Cloden, England, (or Ireland) when it sank along Frying Pan Shoals. Although she purportedly survived the wreck, she ultimately died of starvation.

Donna Ray recalls a story she heard from her high school math teacher, "who was as straight as an arrow when it came to the paranormal." The teacher had been driving back from the Point one night when a cold chill unexpectedly swept through her and the air became pungent with a raw, musty stench. Moments later, a translucent white apparition resembling a woman flew across the road in front of her cart, causing her to slam on the brakes. After the spirit drifted off into the dunes, the air warmed up again and the smell faded away.

What Donna's teacher saw that night is believed to have been the ghost of Theodosia, a local legend among the Bald Head Island community. Kellie Terrell remembers her family keeping their eyes peeled for the ghost of Theodosia.

The story goes that Theodosia Burr Alston, the daughter of Aaron Burr (the third vice president of the United States), was on a schooner heading from Georgetown, South Carolina, to New York when it sank off of Bald Head Island. It's believed that Theodosia drowned since her body was never recovered, although there are several other theories.[22]

Of course, not all of Bald Head Island's legends involve ghosts. Many center around pirates, both real and imagined.

In the seventeenth and eighteenth centuries, when ships ran aground on Frying Pan Shoals, the pirates lying in wait on Bald Head Island would attack the ships, plunder their cargo, and kill everyone on board. It is believed that many buccaneers buried their treasure on BHI and that the island regularly served as a hideout for such notable pirates as Stede Bonnet and Edward Teach (a.k.a. "Blackbeard"). In a nod to those days of yore, two of Bald Head Island's streets are named after these two marauders.[23] And of course, lots of legends emerged.

Pat Thomas, for example, concocted a funny story about the huge mosquitoes on the island. His daughter Leslie tells the tale: "If you hear a *thud, thud, thud* like footsteps, it's the peg-leg mosquito coming up the steps to get you."

In keeping with the pirate theme, Keith Bradley recalls taking his children and their friends out in the extreme darkness of the island in search of "pirate eyes" along the fourth fairway, "before the rise of video games and the disappearance of adventure and innovative challenges."

With extinguished flashlights in hand, they would quietly round the dog leg. Upon a quiet command so as not to spook the pirates, they would simultaneously turn on the flashlights, revealing white shining pirate eyes behind the green and among the trees.

In reality, the eyes belonged to roosting ibis, the long-legged wading birds native to the island, but, to imaginative children, they'd just discovered the hiding places of raiders and buccaneers.

As Pat Miller says, "We're living with memories of nobles and scalawags."

---

[22] Hunter Ingram, "Lost at Sea? The Tragic Mystery of Theodosia Burr Alston," StarNews Online, June 21, 2020, https://www.starnewsonline.com/story/special/2020/06/21/lost-at-sea-tragic-mystery-of-theodosia-burr-alston/113365064/.

[23] "Pirates Invade Bald Head Island," Bald Head Island Limited, July 22, 2015, https://www.baldheadisland.com/blog/2015/7/pirates-invade-bald-head-island.

Chapter 41
The Car Bar

Van Eure recalls spending several weekends at the Bald Head Inn with her parents while they tried to decide which lot to buy. "My dad felt like it needed to be done by swimming in the ocean," she says. So, the family would swim a stretch of 100 yards along the beach and come ashore to investigate the land for a bit—then swim another stretch—until they finally found the perfect location.

It would take much thought and several years before their dream house would be complete. The Eures loved to entertain and, of course, with Thad being a restauranteur (the owner of Raleigh's famous Angus Barn steakhouse), their large kitchen featured the latest commercial appliances.

Having built in the early 1980s, before the Mitchells bought the island, they just missed admittance to the Generator Society. "BHI was Gilligan's Island back then," Van says, referring to the incredible creativity and ingenuity of its residents.

Creativity was something that the Eures also possessed, having built the island's first and only "car bar." The vehicle was decked out with liquor-bottle holders and mixers and ice for cocktails … as well as fishing equipment.

Thad could often be found wearing a Hawaiian shirt and a captain's hat, driving around the island making people drinks out of the car bar. "BHI was the only place that my parents really, truly relaxed," Van says. "They worked so hard their whole lives and when my dad would come down to the island, he became a completely different person."

Thad Eure serving cocktails from his "car bar."
Photo courtesy of Harriet and Cindy Poole.

Chapter 42
The Bench Without an Arm

One day in 1981, with her husband at work and the kids off to school, Beth Kapil opened the morning paper in Raleigh and discovered an article about Bald Head Island, which she'd never heard of even though she was from North Carolina.

Intrigued, she picked up the phone and called the developer, made an appointment, and drove down there that very morning by herself. She met with Buck Timberlake, bought a lot, and drove back to Raleigh in time for dinner.

That night, when her husband, Vijay, asked, "What did you do today?" she responded, "We bought a lot on Bald Head Island." They started building their house five years later, in October 1986, and moved in over Easter weekend of '87.

Initially they were just weekenders, catching the nine o'clock ferry on a Friday night and returning on the three o'clock Sunday ferry. They had only one close neighbor back then, the Bernes—right across the fairway at the edge of the lagoon. The rest of the Generator Society was scattered throughout the island.

There wasn't a club to belong to at that point, but if you bought a lot in 1981, you received a "founding social membership." When the clubhouse was eventually built, these founders automatically became social members.

After Vijay passed away years later, their Bald Head Island friend Brooks Powell took Beth and her family the requisite two miles out to sea to scatter Vijay's ashes over moving water. "Brooks was a true friend and a real character," she says. "He only had part of one arm, which is why the bench outside of the Maritime Market doesn't have an armrest on one side; it was done as a dedication to him."

Beth, like Ann Cathcart, ultimately decided to move to the island as a widow. "I have heard that 10 percent of the women on Bald Head are single," she says. "There are a fair number of single women because it's a great place to be. The women's walking groups are wonderful. We play Mahjong. We establish true friendships."

Many of them also serve their Bald Head Island community. Beth, for example, is a member of the Architectural Review Committee and remains part of the Public Service Auxiliary, which serves and assists first responders during emergencies and was founded by Billie Jean Berne. The auxiliary also conducts fundraisers such as the annual chili supper to purchase necessary equipment not covered in the budget. "All of the positions were a labor of love," Billie Jean says. "A community spirit that lived within us."

Chapter 43
You'll Get a Lot of Reading Done

Tori Cockman has no fonder memories than those of her childhood, adolescence, and adulthood on Bald Head Island.

Her mother's dad—her grandfather, James Draden Moore V (known to most islanders as Draden but whom she fondly called "Papa")—was an accomplished man of many talents. When RCA Records offered Draden the option of early retirement at age sixty, he chose to establish a post-retirement career as a real estate agent on BHI thanks to the continual encouragement of his friend Buck Timberlake, who was already an established real estate agent there.

So, Draden and his wife, Carol, uprooted their lives in Atlanta and moved to Southport in 1980. At the time, the island was still so sparsely populated that Barry Plankers, a fellow realtor on BHI, welcomed Draden by saying, "You'll get a lot of reading done."

It would seem Draden dismissed the comment since he soon became successful at not only selling homes on the island but also befriending the community. He quickly grew to love the island, its history, and all it represented. In fact, he was known to gift his clients at closing with a copy of one of two books about the island available at that time, in which he would write, "To help you appreciate our island even more —Draden."

Tori and her sister were always excited when their parents traveled because then they got to tag along with their grandparents on the island. One of Tori's best memories during that time was when she would ride around in one of the "big carts" (a six-seater golf cart) with her papa. "Papa waved to everyone and everyone waved back," she says. When they returned to his office at the BHI Marina, she would run up the stairs and help herself to some jellybeans from the BHI-monogrammed glass jar he kept on his desk. She also remembers when her grandparents adopted a turtle nest and sponsored a lighthouse step during Old Baldy's restoration fundraiser.

When she visits the Village Chapel today, the light shining through the beautiful Timberlake memorial window reminds her of the richness of God's love and grace toward her family and the island. "Our little haven on BHI creates an unbreakable family bond," she says. "I love that my cousins and I are another generation able to enjoy Bald Head Island, a place that we can all share and enjoy; a place to never take for granted."

It's a legacy she will soak up like the sunshine and salt air.

Chapter 44
A Golf Cart that Died … and a Dog that Didn't

Doug Anderson and his wife came over to BHI for the first time in 1983 to tour the island. They were met by Donnie Copeland, a real estate agent new to BHI who was himself still learning his way around.

"He had a fun, easy-come, easy-go attitude that made looking at properties enjoyable," Doug recalls.

Donnie also had a run-down golf cart. As they started up the hill at West Bald Head Wynd on their way back to the sales office, the golf cart, in true BHI spirit, gave out.

"There we were in what seemed like 100-degree heat, walking back the rest of the way," Doug says, laughing.

Despite all of that—not to mention the fact they hadn't come to the island intending to buy—they purchased a villa that same day.

Advertisement for the new Villas. Courtesy of Bald Head Island newsletter, 1982.

When staying at the villa, they brought their dog along. Accustomed to always being with its owners, the dog became distraught one time when it awoke from a nap upstairs and couldn't find them. Disoriented and in a hurry, the dog ran out the upstairs balcony door and fell off the roof.

"He was badly hurt," Doug recalls, "but the beautiful people at the marina started up a ferry for him and we got him to a veterinary surgeon in Wilmington in time. He lived another fifteen years."

Bald Head Island Villas in 1983. Photo courtesy of Carol and Draden Moore.

Malcolm Fleming sailing through the Villas. Photo courtesy of Sharon Lightbourne.

Chapter 45
On the Fine Art of Gillnetting

The following humorous instruction guide was penned by Pat Thomas in August 1985. It appears in its entirety as originally written:

The fine art of gillnetting at Bald Head, once learned, can provide many hours of enjoyment, fellowship, and family fun. Interesting and sometimes surprising catches, as well as fresh seafood, can be the pleasant result.

The equipment required is not exactly "high tech." A typical gillnetting expedition will, of course, require a gill net. And the common mistake to make is to buy one too long rather than too short. A manageable net is 6-feet high and no more than 75-feet long. The more durable nets are made of #6 monofilament, with lead weights on the bottom and approximately 4-inch plastic net floats on top. Most lead and float lines are of polypropylene. A wide variety of mesh sizes is available, but for the recreational gillnetter a mesh of 1¾–2" x 2" is ideal. Cost of a net is on the order of $45 as available from Memphis Net and Twine, Box 8331, Memphis, TN, phone 800-238-6380.[24]

In addition, the reasonably well-equipped weekend netter will need:

- ¼" yellow polypropylene line (75 feet) "X" feet longer than the net
- Small anchor (Danforth Dinghy)
- 7" x 1" dowel
- Round concrete weight (more later), 25 pound
- 40-gallon plastic trash can
- Large Igloo cooler
- Beer (varying quantities and brands)
- Large float (2 or 3 Clorox bottles)
- Net mending needle
- 1 bottle of Adolph's meat tenderizer
- 3" peg

Optional:

- Jon boat or truck inner tube
- 4" x 4" piece of canvas

---

[24] Believe it or not, this company remains in operation today and this phone number is still one of their working numbers. However, their website provides a different mailing address; it is presumed that the cost of nets has increased. Memphis Net & Twine, accessed February 10, 2022, https://www.memphisnet.net/.

Having collected all of the above gear and figured out how to transport it on your golf cart, head for the beach. The water you want to head for should ideally be dark or muddy. If you watch your net after it is set, you will soon see why unclear water is best. As you will recall, fish have eyes, and upon seeing a net in their path will more often than not jump over it.

As you have figured out by now, the 40-gallon plastic trash can is a magnificent receptacle for toting and storing a gill net. You will soon learn that loading a gill net into the trash can will, if done carefully, produce dividends next time you want to use it.

You are now at the beach—at *early part of rising tide*, mind you. You have at hand this rather absurd collection of materials. You have picked an area of turbid water and have even lucked upon a part of the beach which will, on the rising tide, provide a parallel slough. The big moment is almost at hand. Here are a few of the final "get-in-ready moves" which should be performed with some grace and adroitness.

First

Tie the round concrete anchor or weight to the lead line end which is going to go to sea. Next, fix your large net float (Clorox bottles or better) to the end of the seaward float line. The large float is primarily for the purpose of maintaining visual contact with the seaward end of your net after it is set, so it will not necessarily have to be Clorox.

Second

You have had the presence of mind to cut ¼" wide x ½" deep slot in each end of your 7"x 1" dowel because you guessed that it would be used to spread the beach end of the gill net to keep the lead and float lines from tangling as the tide rises. Make the dowel fast to both lead and float lines in such a way as to spread the two apart and keep them that way during the thrashing it will receive from the surf.

Third

Attach the 75' polypropylene line to the beach end of the float line. Tie the small boat anchor to the lead line. Now take the bitter end of the 75' polypropylene line and tie it to the haft of the small boat anchor as a trip line. (That is to trip the anchor—not you.) By now, I am sure you have learned not to walk on the gill net barefoot, which has nothing to do with the above referenced trip line.

Fourth

Depending on the water temperature and basically your personal choice, you may select one of the two or none of the optional modes of transportation seaward: the inner tube; the john boat [sic]; or none of the above. The third option is best selected when you are 7½' tall. Failing such height, it is recommended that you leave your hat ashore, as the water you will be working towards is on the order of 6–7' deep. If you have selected the inner tube, head for the water with it in hand along with the concrete weight and large float, pulling the net with you.

Fifth

Surely you remembered to invite some family and friends, as it is required, as a measure of your skill and cunning, to have some recipients of the catch lined up in advance—not to mention net pickers (more on that honorable profession later). The object now is for those onshore to pay out the net (they need to pull it along with you) as you wend your way seaward, with the inner tube supplying floating assistance for the weight. Once you're past the breakers you've got it made, if your beach hands keep you unburdened of the weight of the net. If there is a current, hopefully you angled into it from the base of beach operations; or even better yet, you started into the water "up current." Continue making your way seaward until you have stretched it out full length 90 degrees to the beach and with the onshore end up at the edge of the water. If you have walked until your hat floated away, you are not 7½' tall and you have missed part of the instructions—go back. Drop the float, drop the concrete weight. The float will float, the weight will not. (*Exercise care not to get tangled in the net due to the potential for serious, hazardous, and undesirable results.*)

Return to the beach quickly because with a bit of forethought the beer should have had time to chill thoroughly in the large Igloo cooler. You did bring ice?

Sixth

Not yet on the beer! Please take the yellow line back up on the beach after you have adjusted the anchor in keeping with the net's reaction to the current. Did you set the small boat anchor? If not, do so, stretching the lead line out nicely. Now we get to use the peg. Drive it into the sand at a point well above the high-water mark. You might use the concrete weight as a hammer, but hopefully it is not now available for this purpose.

Now for the beer!

Things to watch for:

1. The largest fish jumping over the set net.
2. Your net drifting (your weight is gone or too light or too much surf).
3. Boaters from Southport who use the middle of the net as a target or who raid it for bait.
4. Industrial quantities of sea lettuce, sargassum, or floating marsh grass, which are all good for many hours of enjoyable net cleaning.
5. The knowledgeable net pickers who drift away from the beach towards the end of the beer but before the net is pulled in.
6. The lead and float lines [tangling] in the surf.

If your timing was good and you set the net on mid-rising tide, six hours later on mid-falling tide you are ready to see and harvest the fruits of your labor.

If for any reason the sea still covers your beach anchor, a tug on the appropriate end of the yellow line will trip the anchor. You begin to haul the net onto the beach. We are certain that you have found an ideal place which is devoid of sticks, snags, and marsh grass which has carefully waited to tangle itself in your new net.

It is about now that you find that your concrete weight really weighs a lot more than it did when you took it out. As you haul it in, carefully coil and put the yellow line in the bottom of your garbage can. As you pull in net, load it into the trash can after you have picked the net clean. There is an optional method which entails stretching the net out over the wet area of the beach to pick it and then loading it into the trash can. But the more important part of the program is picking the net. (Refer to item 5 of the list of things to watch out for.)

Fish can be terribly clever in getting snagged in your net. With a little practice you can learn how to push them on through the mesh or work them out backwards, freeing their gills from the monofilament line. Gloves of the cotton work variety are most helpful. It is along about here that you should wonder about the Adolph's meat tenderizer. Sometimes the remnants of a Portuguese man-of-war may be encountered in your net. When it begins to burn, rub some wet sand on the afflicted area, wash off the sand, and then rub on the meat tenderizer. It should bring the unpleasant problem to a quick halt.

Load your fish in your Igloo cooler, have a fish fry, give them away to friends, use them for bait, and be prepared to do it again.

Your catch may consist of: flounder, horse mackerel, spot, bluefish, mullet, pompano (always in the net close to the beach), weak fish (trout), and sharks. In certain months (August–September) you will load up on small sharks but later in the early fall (late Sept/Oct/Nov) your catch will be of preponderantly better quality. It is a lot of fun and will provide many hours of fellowship and many coolers of good fish.

On Concrete Weights

A superior deep-water weight can be made by pouring Sacrete (watered and mixed, of course) into a round or roundish form approximately 3" or 4" thick and 18" in diameter. While the cement is still liquid, place a piece of ¼" diameter reinforcement bar into the center—bent into a "U" or omega shape. The steel loop will provide you with a hitch point for tying the lead line of your gill net. By forming the weight in a smooth and rounded shape there is less tendency to snag and generally get caught up in your net. It is also somewhat easier on your legs as you are required to bump it several times as you go out to set the net.

On Advanced Gillnetting

A derivation of gillnetting bordering on "high tech" calls for the placement of a permanent anchor placed seaward to which is attached a pulley of some relatively corrosion-proof material. Through this pulley you run a permanent sea-to-shore ¼" line. This line is bridled to the seaward end of the gill net, then allowing for a winnable tug-of-war, with the prize being a somewhat easily set gill net.

Advantages of this system are:

1. You can set it almost alone.
2. It is very nice in December through February.
3. It is relatively unaffected by current.

Disadvantages are:

1. It is a conventional source for people who happen by and need a piece of rope.
2. It is lonesome.
3. It is not conducive to volume beer drinking.
4. The developer may wish to minimize this sort of activity.
5. You can't go looking for the murkiest of waters.

PART V: THE LEGACY

"There's not a spot on the island that I go, that I don't have sweet, sweet memories. This island, the residents here, we are a family. The island feels like a blanket of love that continues to wrap me."
—Pat Miller

Nature & Conservancy

Chapter 46
The Lure of the Landscape

Without a doubt, the unique landscape of Bald Head Island was—and remains—its primary attraction. It has the distinction of being the northernmost semitropical location in the country where trunk palms, such as the Sabal palm tree, grow naturally, and it is host to a disparate yet interconnected marsh, forest, and beach. Together, they offer a spectacularly rare habitat for wildlife and humans alike.

A wide variety of flora also flourishes on the island. Leslie Thomas loves all the resurrection ferns in the live oak trees, whereas Bill Berne is irritated by the plethora of poison ivy.

Nevertheless, "the beauty of BHI is overwhelming," says Gene Douglas, who was particularly fond of the incredibly tall dunes along South Beach in the early days. Over the years, the dune structure has eroded, undoubtedly quickened when the Corps of Engineers deepened the shipping channel. Despite attempts at beach renourishment, the dunes never regained their former glory. Yet to this day, every time Alex Mitchell sees those dunes in the distance, perched on the other side of the marsh, it resonates with him like nothing else. "It feels so magnificent; it feels like hope," he says.

The island's pristine beauty and seclusion during the pioneer years offered equal measures of tranquility, excitement, and romance to its visitors and residents. "Back when Plunkett and I first came," recalls Harper Peterson, "Muscadine Wynd was the end of the earth. Everything from there to East Beach until you got to *Captain Charlie's* was so remote and untouched."

Expansive, secluded South Beach with the Dunlap house in the background. Photo courtesy of Melinda Freeman.

South Beach from *Milbo Hilton*. Photo courtesy of Sharon Lightbourne.

"The lure of the beach, and the promises of privacy and beauty, far outweighed the problems encountered," Pat Cunningham explains.

Marshall Dunlap shares that perspective. He often preferred to explore by himself, which was a good thing because it was not uncommon to take long walks on the beach without encountering a single other person.

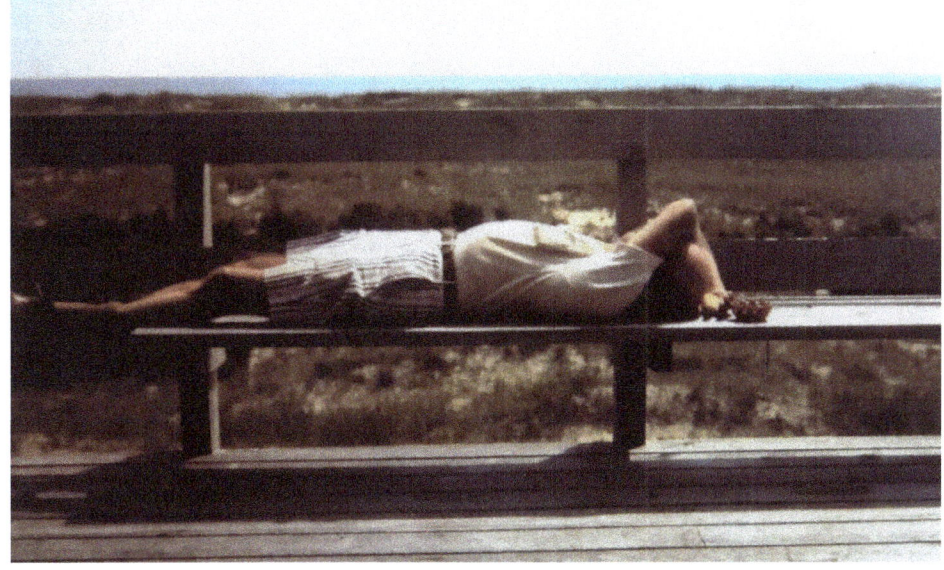

Bo Caperton enjoying some quiet time on his porch. Photo courtesy of Sharon Lightbourne.

Cindy Poole appreciated the opportunity to worship during such uninterrupted walks. "There was no mistaking the existence of a wondrous God when walking the beach early in the mornings or when witnessing breathtaking sunsets," she says. "He was always right there."

The Crowells also enjoyed long walks on the beach at night, when they could alternately search for the elusive ghost crab and study the starry skies to identify constellations.

Stargazing was something everyone appreciated in the days when there was very little light pollution.

Kellie Terrell could often be found sitting on the deck after dinner, covered in bug spray, looking at stars because the generator was often out. Patricia Young walked her dog by the light of the Milky Way during its season. And Keith and Merry Bradley enjoyed tremendous views of the constellations through a friend's telescope.

A direct correlation to all of this seclusion, of course, is freedom.

"The underdevelopment and the wildness of that island fit my dad very, very well because there were no rules," says Leslie Thomas. "He told me when I moved down to Hilton Head that I wouldn't be happy down there because it's 'not real.' Bald Head Island in the beginning was real; it wasn't developed or commercialized. You could do whatever you wanted on the island and that was part of the beauty of that time period. That's why it was perfect for my parents then. Dad wouldn't stand for the rules of Bald Head Island now."

Despite the addition of more homes, businesses, and rules, BHI's landscape has nevertheless retained its original appeal. "The splendor of the island is spectacular," says Doug Anderson. "The island is changing, but it's still remote and nature-oriented compared to other places on the East Coast."

Harriet Poole and her dog, Smokey, on a sandy Bald Head Island road in 1976. Photo courtesy of Harriet and Cindy Poole.

Chapter 47
Critters for Company

When you're approaching Bald Head Island, it's usually the birds you'll see first. Seagulls swoop toward the ferry, ready to catch breadcrumbs tossed by tiny hands. Brown pelicans fly in formation low over the water, ready to dive and catch their next meal. Along the banks of the lagoons or in the marshland, the stark contrast of snowy egrets and white ibis stand out among the green and beige hues of the grasses around them. Great blue herons stand perched on docks and trees, and the large nests of ospreys can be seen atop channel markers and dock pilings.

BHI has served as a haven to a wide variety of bird species ranging from wood ducks and bald eagles to mockingbirds and, perhaps most notably, the colorful painted buntings. In the spring, when the buntings return from their southern migration, they can be heard singing and chirping as they flit among the dense foliage—and are admired as they descend upon bird feeders in yards like Beth Kapil's. Beth loves the painted buntings and hummingbirds that frequent the multiple bird baths she places in her yard every summer. "They are quite smart, little creatures," she says.

Indeed they are. And, like the residents they get seed from, birds often have personalities of their own.

Watts Carr recalls the tricolored heron that once befriended his wife, Betsy, as she was surfcasting on the beach. The almost mystical bird stayed close by for a few hours, allowing Betsy to take some great photos. The next day, Betsy returned to her fishing spot and discovered the heron waiting for her. It came within twenty feet of her, and she shared shrimp bait and some of her catch with it. The third day, it had disappeared, never to return. But Watts considered the bird to be "almost human" since it stood almost 5′ tall and was alarmingly comfortable with Betsy. Indeed, the animals of Bald Head Island and its residents seemed to experience an innate connection.

Plunkett Dodge recalls being in the water when five dolphins appeared within a few feet of her and her companions. "We reached out and they touched our hands as they swam by," she says. "It was just magical."

Harper Peterson shared a similar experience but on land. As he was walking his property before it was cleared, a ten-point buck stepped out of the foliage across from him. After a few moments of them silently staring at each other, the buck turned and walked the other way.

It was this ability to experience wildlife in their natural environment that motivated Eleanor Cosgrove to preserve "the Point." Her son Chris remembers the fundraiser called "Get the Point" that his mom and several other residents spearheaded. "They were able to purchase the land from the developers so it remained a protected sanctuary for both humans and animals."

Hidden in Plain View

Wildlife was everywhere on Bald Head Island, whether the pioneers and outfitters were aware of it or not.

Sometimes, due to their small size or natural camouflage, the animals were heard more than seen, especially at night after the generators were turned off. Eleanor Cosgrove and Kellie Terrell recall how the evening air was filled with a chorus of frogs and crickets that wafted through the open windows.

While such outdoor nocturnal music might lull one to sleep, noises emanating from within a house tends to keep one awake. Donna Ray recalls the time her family stayed in a house down by the creek and experienced an unrestful night's sleep due to the sound of mice running around all night long. The next morning, to their horror, they discovered mice droppings littering their pillows and blankets. Such rodent behavior apparently didn't horrify one of Robin and Barbara Hayes' guests, though, who supposedly wore her glasses to bed "so she could better see the mice as they ran over her."

Harriet Poole often had the privilege of dealing with mice in the daytime. After one too many experiences of field mice scattering as she opened the oven door, she took to kicking her oven before attempting to cook on the stove.

Snakes, too, were well known for surprising islanders in unexpected places.

Patricia Young called Island Security on the CB for help the time she was alone and found a snake curled up in an open suitcase on the bedroom floor. Then there was the time a small snake wound itself around the bathroom doorknob—with her mother inside. Alerted by her mother's thin wail, Patricia bravely grabbed a rake and broom and managed to expel it from the house.

Beth Kapil remembers the time her husband, Vijay, called her from the kitchen to come look at something in their bathroom. Upon her arrival, she was shocked to witness a rat snake crawling out of the sink. Her initial reaction was to put the house on the market, but Vijay convinced her to stay after he solved the problem by covering the pipe with mesh. While snakes never made another appearance inside the house, Beth soon realized the reptiles still lurked outdoors.

One Memorial Day weekend as Beth walked up her driveway she saw a snake eight inches in diameter and so long that it covered the entire width of the driveway. "I almost had a heart attack," she said. And just in case you think she might be exaggerating, she adds, "The neighbors across the street saw it, too."

As discussed thus far, Bald Head Island is home to creatures that are beautiful to look at, relaxing to listen to, and sometimes frightening to discover. Yet there are many more animals on the island. Some that make the islanders look at them in awe and respect, some that cause frustration and laughter, and some that outright need assistance.

Carolyn Fleming feeding a squirrel. Photo courtesy of Sharon Lightbourne.

The Predators

Plunkett Dodge was out for a jog, running down Federal Road, when a fox popped out of the forest and literally ran along beside her—just like a pet dog out jogging with its owner. Surprised by this unusual behavior, Plunkett was, on the one hand, worried that it might be rabid and was going to bite her leg. On the other hand, she found it thrilling. Before she could think anything more about it, the fox dipped back into the woods, leaving Plunkett with a memory she would long treasure.

Another predator is more frequently sighted throughout the island. One that isn't small, cute, and furry but rather, large, menacing, and scaly. That predator is the American alligator.

Since alligators are a common sight, it might come as a surprise to learn that Charlotte Dunlap didn't believe her cousin when she claimed there was a large alligator between Charlotte's house and the beach. "This was back in the days when we had a long stretch of high dunes and sea oats between our house and the ocean," Charlotte explains. "I assured my cousin that it was impossible for an alligator to be there because they lived in the lagoon, not in the ocean."

The man in the picture is dwarfed by the large dune scrub and vast grassy beach. Photo courtesy of Donna Ray.

The Wesley House   South Beach   Bald head Island   1987

Dunes were once high enough to partially obstruct the view of the homes behind them. This was the Wesley House on South Beach in 1987. Photo courtesy of Nancy Giacci.

Yet when Charlotte went outside, she discovered that there most certainly was an alligator … almost at the bottom of her steps. She quickly radioed the island's security guards, who promptly arrived in their pick-up truck with rope.

"They were scared to death of the gator—and he was fierce, hissing and swishing that huge tail," Charlotte recalls. But the two men, being cheered on by all the ladies drinking cocktails on the deck, had no choice but to brave the beast. By all accounts, they put on a fine show. Repeatedly they attempted to lasso the reptile; once it almost made an escape under the house, and another time it hid under the Dunlap's Jeep. Yet they persevered until they were finally able to rope it and drive it to a lagoon, where it swam away.

Watts Carr shares a similar encounter. He was at home, loading golf clubs on his cart in preparation for a nine-hole outing, when he heard a loud *WHAP!* And then another *WHAP!* Deciding to investigate the unusual sound, Watts looked under the house and discovered a ten- to twelve-foot alligator slamming its tail against one of the pilings. Watts ran upstairs, cussing the whole way, and called the police. Betsy and Watts watched out the window as the gator continued to smack the piling until the police arrived. "They told us to go on and play our round of golf," Watts says. "So we did as we were told. We played nine, came home, and the gator was gone."

It hadn't been caught, though. Unable to rope the large reptile, the police had badgered it until it finally went up and over the dune and across the beach to the river. "He stayed out there on the beach and in the water for three days before finally going away," Watts says.

Unfortunately, not everyone has an innate respect for—and fear of—alligators. Watts recalls another time when he was sitting on his deck, admiring the view, when he noticed a woman and two young kids walk to a nearby pond. Watts watched in astonishment as they sat down on the bank, their feet almost in the water, and proceeded to tie a chicken neck to the end of a fishing rod. "So there was this woman with what looked to be maybe a six-year-old and an eight-year-old, trying to lure an alligator with a chicken neck!" Watts exclaims incredulously.

In an attempt to protect them, he yelled down at her to leave the area because fishing wasn't allowed, much less gator "fishing," to which she replied, "No gator is gonna get a kid of mine!" So as they continued to sit there, Watts rushed to call 911. "The police were there in three minutes," he recalls. "They forcibly jerked her and the kids away just as a large alligator came up out of the lagoon and onto the bank where they had been sitting."

Beth Kapil's alligator story depicts just how fortunate the previous woman and her children had been.

It was a beautiful summer day and Beth was sitting out on her porch reading when she heard a splash. Glancing up from her book, she saw that a dog belonging to the family across the fairway had jumped into the lagoon. As it splashed around, having fun and cooling off, Beth knew it was in danger and couldn't just sit there and watch. As she started across the fairway to warn the family, she noticed Billie Jean Berne coming out of her house to do the same. "And at that point," Beth says, "the dog jumped out of the lagoon and an alligator jumped out after it, managing to take a little nip out of the dog's rear end."

The dog was wounded but he survived. The alligator sulked.

"That alligator sat in the water staring at that house for days hoping that dog would come back," she says. "I've seen zillions of alligators on the island but that's the first time I've ever seen one actually jump—he was in the air. They say they can jump half the length of their body, and he did."

The Scavengers

One animal on Bald Head Island that might surprise people is the wild hog. Back in the 1930s, farmers were encouraged to raise hogs and cattle on the island, but the effort was abandoned a decade later when the military set up base during WWII. Some of the hogs were left behind during the transition and learned to survive on their own.[25]

Charles Young recalls taking trips over to the island in the 1960s specifically to hunt the wild hogs, and Cindy Poole heard rumors of wild hogs weighing up to 1,000 pounds. But Jeff Cosgrove and his brothers survived to tell the tale of a run-in with a big, wild pig named Gertrude. "One time my brothers and I were hanging out, walking around. When we turned the corner of our house, Chris ran face-to-face into Gertrude. They both ran in opposite directions."

While property owners may have had only fleeting encounters with wild hogs, it seems everyone on Bald Head Island held long-term, up-close-and-personal relationships with raccoons.

"There was a time when you really couldn't leave anything where a raccoon couldn't get to it," says Mrs. Dale Georgaide. "They were everywhere. They would come up on our back deck and watch us watching TV. One time, one of our guests left a golf bag outside with some crackers in the pocket. A raccoon chewed a hole in the bag to get to them."

Ann Cathcart lives in a villa right on the beach, with a deck that faces South Beach and offers an unobstructed view of the road leading to the club. Every night, she and her husband would sit on the deck to watch the sunset as they enjoyed a glass of wine and appetizers. And every evening one summer, two fat raccoons would waddle along the road all the way up to the club. "Their timing was perfect," Ann recalls. "We would

---

[25] "Bald Head Island History," accessed February 15, 2022. https://www.baldheadisland.com/about/bald-head-island-history.

watch them go around the side of the club to the back where the dumpster was. We couldn't see the dumpster, of course, but we knew what they were doing and by the time we were through with our wine and hors d'oeuvres, here they came, waddling back after their dinner in the dumpster. It happened every evening that summer; they must have had a permanent reservation at the club."

Patricia Young recalls one particular evening after the Generator Society's annual surf fishing contest, which was the origins of today's BHI Fishing Rodeo. "I had caught a doozer, a real doozer of a fish," she says with pride. Knowing better than to leave the potential prize-winning fish in the cooler on the ground or in the cart outside, she and her husband carried the cooler to the upstairs deck for safekeeping until they could enter the fish in the contest the next morning.

At some point in the middle of the night, Patricia heard a loud noise. "We looked out and saw a raccoon had pushed the cooler off the deck, which crashed on the ground. And he was running away with my fish!" Determined to get her fish back, Patricia flew down the stairs and out the door, tracking the critter through the dunes in her pajamas by moonlight. Despite her best efforts, the raccoon won after she lost the fish-tail trail in the dune bushes some distance away from the house. Her fish was gone.

It's probably safe to assume that Patricia harbored a grudge against raccoons after that frustrating experience. Which is why she most likely experienced some measure of satisfaction from the next raccoon encounter.

One night, Patricia's Golden Retriever, Sunny, began barking incessantly, so she let her out. After Sunny continued to bark for several minutes, Patricia went out to investigate and discovered that Sunny had run a raccoon up to the top of the flagpole in their front yard. "I couldn't get Sunny to come in because she would just bark from inside, so she stayed out there until dawn." The raccoon, "treed" all night, finally escaped in the morning.

But sometimes the raccoons *did* make it inside the homes. And that's when mayhem really struck.

Plunkett Dodge, while still living at *Captain Charlie's*, remembers hosting a big family meal with twelve people gathered around the table. She noticed her dad kept brushing something away from his lap during dinner. "Finally, he looked down and saw that it wasn't one of our dogs under the table but a raccoon!" Upon his announcement, everyone jumped up and started yelling as they rushed to get a broom to shoo it away.

Millie Caperton McVey recalls raccoons eating through screen doors to gain access to their house. But occasionally the animals lucked out when a human inadvertently provided a grand entrance.

Such was the case the time the Pooles neglected to close an upstairs sliding glass door before they left the island. When they returned three weeks later, they discovered the kitchen in complete disarray. "Every drawer and cupboard in the kitchen was opened and the entire contents of each was scattered on the floor," Frank recalls. "It took eight garbage bags to contain the mess and $800 to repair the damage." Adding insult to injury, that $800 (the equivalent of $2,300 today) wasn't insurable.

Some of the mess the raccoons left behind after their exploration of the *Tree House*. Photo courtesy of Harriet and Cindy Poole.

The raccoon damage warranted an article about it. Photo courtesy of BHI Association's *Bald Head Island* newsletter, summer 1983. Photographer: Kelly Carlton.

Sometimes the voracious raccoons invited friends to join them.

As if Patricia Young didn't already have enough critter stories, this one centers around the night she and Charlie heard a noise in the kitchen. "We came out to find a raccoon sitting on one end of the dining table munching on some bread, and an opossum merrily chomping on Styrofoam at the other end of the table," she says. The raccoon skedaddled as soon as he was caught red-handed but the ornery opossum required some encouragement from a broom handle before he took off.

Yet perhaps not all the blame should fall on the mischievous raccoons alone. After all, it appeared that in the daytime, many islanders set the stage for such nighttime escapades.

Ainsley Dunlap feeds a raccoon as Wick Dunlap watches. Photo courtesy of Marshall Dunlap.

According to Marshall Dunlap, one of the islander traditions was luring raccoons up onto their porches, sometimes even into the house, with scraps of food. "The raccoons would eat right out of their hands, almost like dogs; they were like pets," he says.

Leslie Thomas agrees. "My mother had a pet raccoon. Not really, but it frequented the house so often that Mother would leave food out for him and he would eat at the front door." She even named him Captain Charlie, after Captain Charlie Swan, the lightkeeper.

Regardless of how frustrating—and costly—the raccoons could be, there were a few individuals who looked out for their health and safety.

Donna Ray remembers how George and Martha Hayworth worked to rescue juvenile raccoons on the island following Hurricane Diana in 1984, the first major storm to hit the East Coast in twenty years. Facing severe flooding that lasted for weeks, Martha took in the orphaned raccoons and raised them until they became too aggressive to handle. "She invented an entire system for taking care of them," Donna says. "She bottle-fed them and even held them over the toilet with a small cotton ball on their stomach to help them pass waste. It was as admirable as it was fascinating."

Donna's children loved going to Martha's house and helping to feed the baby raccoons. "It's something that could never happen nowadays, but back then, nobody had a problem with it," Donna says. "That's just the way things were."

In similar fashion, Ann Cathcart remembers gathering with friends for dinner and everyone being concerned about Anne Pickering's absence. "She didn't come and she didn't come and she didn't come," Ann says. "She was sort of habitually late because she was always doing good stuff, but she was much later than usual." The group went looking for her and found her on the side of the road—with several orphaned baby opossums. "She took them back to her house where she and Martha Hayworth fed them with eye droppers. They raised this little bunch of opossums until they could be released back into the wild."

Throughout it all, the pioneers and outfitters maintained their sense of humor, epitomized by Harriet Poole and Lee Wester's dinner party at which they served fifteen guests "raccoon stew," which actually consisted of hamburger and various cans of chow mein that they had on hand. But the joke was later turned on them.

After the guests had departed, Harriet heard the dinner bell ringing. Thinking that Thad Wester had returned for something, Frank Poole went to the door and discovered a raccoon standing with the bell handle in its mouth. A chase ensued, and the bell was recovered.

Boundaries

When Marshall Dunlap was a boy, he would often go through the garbage and sort out all the food scraps he could find. He bagged the scraps and drove around the island on what he called a "Critter Ride." The scraps would be dropped at various locations around the island, and later on he would circle back to see all the animals feasting on them: foxes, wolves, raccoons, and anything else that lived in the forest. "It was a great pastime," he says.

Such an activity is highly discouraged these days.

"With all the deer, coyote, foxes, birds, sharks, and porpoises," Pat Miller says, "this island is paradise. But people need to respect the animals by not feeding them, not getting close to them. People need to know that this island, in its own way, is still a wild and primitive place."

Chapter 48
The Conservancy

One animal in particular—the turtle—was the catalyst for what would come to be known as the Conservancy on Bald Head Island. Today the Conservancy is a full-fledged nonprofit organization whose mission is to discover, learn, conserve, and preserve.[26] Although best known for their Sea Turtle Protection Program, they also offer a host of other important educational opportunities and preservation services, including environmental alerts, a 24/7 injured wildlife hotline, and a sustainability/recycling program.

But it hasn't always been that way. "Nowadays, there are guided activities for tourists and residents, but back then people interacted with the turtles as they pleased," Marshall Dunlap says. "It was never organized; it was just a part of daily life. People were always living with and around nature."

Keith and Merry Bradley consider the Conservancy to be a great example of what volunteers can do on the island. "People saw the need and stepped up to fill positions to grow the organization," Keith says. According to James Poole, the Conservancy began in 1983 as a grassroots effort by the residents to first protect the eggs until the turtles hatched, and then help the hatchlings get to the ocean. Becky Bunn is reported to have been the first person on the island to begin covering Loggerhead turtle nests with mesh wire to protect the eggs from fox and raccoons, which earned her the title "Turtle Lady." Bill Berne helped start the Conservancy and was the second president; Thad Wester was the first.

The generator house at *Captain Charlie's* served as an "office." There, a large bulletin board showing the daily tally of turtle hatchings was maintained by volunteers. Island residents were the initial turtle patrollers and nest monitors prior to the Conservancy staff taking over this important activity.

Leslie Thomas was one of those initial volunteers, and later, when the Conservancy efforts became more organized, she also participated in the turtle nest adoptions. "I grew up really admiring the turtles and was intrigued by them," she says. "I think they are iconic creatures, much to be admired and hopefully not to be lost."

Mrs. Dale Georgaide remembers the early turtle walks. "The way it worked then was that you just showed up at *Captain Charlie's* at the appointed time; eleven o'clock p.m., I think. It was really dark on the island at night; there were many more trees and fewer roads than today. Going out Federal Road was creepy, especially when the lights on the golf cart reflected off eyes in the woods, primarily raccoons and foxes."

---

[26] BHI Conservancy, accessed February 10, 2022, https://www.bhic.org/about-us/.

April 16, 1984

Dear Property Owner,

Brace yourself for parenthood!! Won't you be a Foster Parent to some of our Loggerhead turtles and share in the nurture and protection of some of the world's oldest creatures?

The Organizational Meeting for the new Bald Head Conservancy was held at the Inn on March 18th. The details may be read in the enclosed article from The State Port Pilot. The attendance was large, representative and enthusiastic. Because the turtle project instigated by the NC Wildlife Commission, Nature Conservancy, and our Property Owners has been so successful, and because it's on our own "home turf", it seemed time for us to assume the full responsibility for it. We do this with the support and encouragement of the NC Nature Conservancy and its President, Bill De Buys, who will be on our Board of Directors.

The financial responsibility now rests squarely on our shoulders. The Mitchell family has very generously agreed to match our gifts. Thanks to many of you who answered the plea for gifts last fall to fund the '84 project, we now have $4000 toward the needed $10,000 goal. With the Mitchells' matching gift of $10,000, we would have the necessary $20,000 to carry out the turtle program, as well as other exciting activities being planned by Turtle Lady Cindy Meekins and her Education Committee.

At this writing, Cindy is beginning her work on faith alone, since without further gifts, we are unable to even discuss her salary. And this is the time that supplies must be purchased if Cindy and her much needed intern are to ready the nursery in time!

At the March meeting, the Conservancy directors voted to designate gifts at four levels:

Individual Membership	$25
Family Membership	$50
Sponsor (Includes Family)	$100
Patron (Includes Family)	$250 - up

An enclosed letter from Cindy will tell you how you might adopt a turtle nest. You who gave last fall may add to that gift to attain the needed designation.

We are a young organization and there are many interesting plans to make the Bald Head Conservancy special. Many of you will be called on to serve on its various committees. We need, not only your gifts, but your ideas and active participation. Won't you become charter member of the Bald Head Conservancy? Motherhood won't wait!

Sincerely,

Betty Timberlake

Betty Timberlake
Membership Chairman

Gifts to Bald Head Conservancy, Inc. are tax deductible.

Bald Head Conservancy fundraiser to adopt a turtle nest and offset the costs of the Conservancy's projects. Courtesy of Harriet and Cindy Poole.

One August night in the mid-1980s, the head of the Conservancy asked Missy Anderson, Doug Anderson's wife, to lead the turtle walk because she needed to go to the mainland. In late summer, the nests have already been identified; the focus is on ensuring the safe hatching of eggs.

Doug recalls how about thirty people showed up around midnight, with Missy and Doug leading them down East Beach near the Point. After walking extensively until

1:30 or 2:00 a.m., everyone was getting tired and irritated. "Missy and I felt quite a bit of pressure on us as the organizers to find an active nest and we weren't finding anything." Just as they were about to give up, they came upon a nest that was "boiling"—a term used when a nest is percolating with hatchlings starting to come out.

"We got down on our hands and knees, all thirty of us, and began to make a path for them to get down the beach to the water," he recalls. "There were about 150 of these beautiful little baby turtles. It was life changing."

Needless to say, everyone went home happy after that.

In another incident, Ann Cathcart recalls when a nesting turtle got caught in a deep tidal pool down by the Point. "She had been stuck two or three days when the Conservancy intervened. They had been monitoring her and waiting to see if she could escape on her own. But she was too tired and it was too stressful for her, plus she had no access to food."

So the Conservancy put out an urgent message, asking anyone available on the island to come help. "I'll bet a hundred people came down there," Ann says. "I mean, where else would you say, 'We've got to rescue this turtle' and everybody comes? Only on Bald Head Island."

They formed a human chain, holding hands from one side of the tidal pool to the other, and walked from end to end, scooting the turtle to an edge where several interns and some of the firefighters lifted her into a rescue vehicle. She was then transported down the beach, where she made her way into the ocean and swam off. "There was a great big cheer and everybody was so happy," Ann says.

Another notable rescue mission was when a nest hatched in the daylight. "Baby turtles were running across South Bald Head Wynd," Ann recalls. "So we all grabbed our sand buckets and went running down there. Somebody stopped traffic and we all grabbed the little turtles and put them in the buckets and put them in the ocean. It was great."

Currently, the Conservancy is the only nonprofit entity in North Carolina that is permitted to place homing devices on the turtles and track them via satellite.

"Probably the single most important factor in the preservation of BHI was the establishment of the Bald Head Island Conservancy," states Gene Douglas. "The Conservancy provides a constant reminder of how important their function is for the island. I also believe their work, particularly in education, attracted individuals to BHI who were dedicated environmentalists. I must also note that the Mitchell family was a strong supporter of the Conservancy and donated the land where the Conservancy [was] built."

Keith Bradley echoes Gene's sentiments. "I cannot discount the role that Bob and Sylvia Timmons played all over the island—volunteer firemen, nurse/EMT, you name it—but

Bob was especially instrumental in the formation of Smith Island Land Trust [SILT]," he says. This organization, a subsidiary of the Conservancy, acquired individual land donations to create conservation easements, thereby protecting many acres in the maritime forest (under the care of the State of North Carolina) and island beachfront.

SILT's "Save the Cape" fundraiser protected the last remaining cape on the East Coast —Cape Fear. Early fundraising efforts included campfire sing-a-longs and crab fests on the beach, but the majority of funds were raised in order to meet Bald Head Limited's challenge: if SILT raised $1,000 in six months, Limited would give them the eleven acres of land they sought. Donations poured in, ranging from an accumulation of pennies from a school to a single donation of $25,000. The Mitchells held true to their word and donated the Point, the land in front of where the Shoals Club now sits.

Keith himself was active in SILT, helping to locate and plant thousands of grass cultivars along the dunes. The grasses act as a buffer, helping to prevent salt water from infiltrating the lagoons and thereby changing the ecology of the island.

Charlie Young also worked with the Conservancy to establish an enclosed ibis sanctuary to protect the birds' nesting site from development. This is also where Fluffy the thirteen-foot alligator lived for many years.

Fences and gates, of course, arouse curiosity. The gate to the sanctuary was so frequently damaged from people climbing over it that Charlie finally coated it with axle grease to help mitigate the problem. "The first people we caught were on the Conservancy board and they could get a key any time they wanted to," recalls Patricia Young, laughing.

Beach erosion. Photo courtesy of Melinda Freeman.

Pat Miller worries that such environmental dedication will be lost when the Mitchells eventually sell the island and younger residents replace the old guard. "It's scary to think that this new generation may not want what the old generation had. There is a very unique balance here on the island; the Generator Society and the Mitchells knew that. They were tremendous advocates for the ecosystem here and everyone worked very hard to preserve it. If we don't continue to work together, the next generation won't have a special place anymore. Nature should be the focus and we don't want to lose sight of that!"

Keith Bradley concurs. "As a 'second-generation Generator Society' participant, I hope that commercialism will not destroy the island's respite. The Myrtle Beach phenomenon is a threat and is really what we all wanted to escape by investing in BHI. I am glad to say that Merry and I and many of our friends mentioned herein all got to realize what the island was all about."

Ann Cathcart agrees and believes the Conservancy is instrumental in helping to prevent such commercialism and environmental disregard through its emphasis on hands-on education. "I love how attached and enthusiastic people get about the nature on the island," she says. "It's just wonderful to watch and encouraging to see young people be so enthusiastic about the world around them and how it works and what we're doing. It opens their eyes; you feel like you've really helped them look at the world a little differently."

Community & Camaraderie

Chapter 49
Leisurely Lifestyle

Even though the Generator Society wasn't always thrilled with the increased development of the island, they did welcome its burgeoning social scene.

In the early days, entertainment consisted of exploring the island, visiting with fellow property owners, and engaging in whatever books and games they brought with them from the mainland. Children didn't have to worry about being bored. Not only was the island full of adventure, it was also teeming with playmates, especially since each family usually brought along extra kids to adventure with.

They would run races around the sand roads, taking advantage of the wonderful freedom to, as Kellie Terrell says, "explore the island as far as our feet would take us." They went swimming and rafting in the ocean all day, eventually to be called out of the water by parents offering towels and peanut butter and jelly sandwiches. They walked and shelled on the beach for hours with no one else in sight, discovering lots of seashells and some shipwreck parts, which they eagerly collected. Leslie Thomas still possesses a small bottle containing the tiniest sand dollars and starfish she ever found.

Unrestored and unlocked, Old Baldy Lighthouse beckoned children and adults alike. Climbing the rickety steps, sometimes in the dark with flashlights, they made their way to the windowless top where they admired the expansive view.

Bo and Mildred Caperton with their grandchildren on East Beach in 1977. Courtesy of Millie Caperton McVey.

Teenagers learned to drive stick shifts and four-wheel drives on rutted, sandy roads. Later, when cars were banned and electric golf carts became the primary mode of island transportation, they'd sometimes hot-wire carts . . . or get stuck at the beach. "In the early days, golf carts were inefficient," Keith Bradley explains. "You needed to take quarters along with your beach gear in order to charge your cart at the old gazebo for the return trip from East Beach."

Golf cart driving on sandy road. Photo courtesy of Pat and Charlie Young.

East Beach Gazebo. Original artwork by Nancy Giacci.

Golf carts replaced four-wheel drives in the driveways of BHI in the early '80s. Photo courtesy of Harriet and Cindy Poole.

When Alex Mitchell was a teenager, he would take small sailboats and explore the waters surrounding the island. "It was a paradise, with breathtaking open skies stretching far across the horizon as far as you could see," he says. "From the marshes, to the beaches, to the fast-moving waters of the channel, it was such a unique place to adventure in."

The adults gradually transitioned from backyard horseshoes and badminton games to organized tennis and croquet leagues. Cindy Poole played tennis with Kaye Cowher, wife of football coach Bill Cowher of Pittsburgh Steelers fame, while Bill and Billie Jean Berne could frequently be found with mallets in hand, taking aim at Harper Peterson's croquet ball.

By 1989, croquet had gained such interest on the island that a second court (or "greensward") was built, and the first-ever North Carolina State Championship was held at BHI that same year. Bill Berne came in second place at that competition; Harper Peterson later became the U.S. national amateur single champ and club team champ in 1990, and entered the World Croquet Federation Championship in 2016.[27]

---

[27] "Croquet History," The Bald Head Island Club, accessed February 10, 2022, https://www.bhiclub.net/history; "2016 ACWC Entry List," World Croquet Federation, accessed February 10, 2022, https://worldcroquet.org/2016-acwc-entry-list/.

Golf, too, grew in popularity. The original course designed by George Cobb opened for play in 1974 (although James Poole claims to have test-driven a Chevrolet over the course during its construction, slaloming around trees piled up in the middle of the prospective fairways). Bill Berne recalls it as being "a beautiful golf course all to yourself, and if you didn't like the way you played a hole, you could turn around and play it over." The Dunlaps also loved the "quiet and stunning golf course that was so often without players."

Fairway view from the Old Baldy Lighthouse. Photo courtesy of Carol and Draden Moore.

Two unidentified golfers tee off at the Bald Head Island golf course. Courtesy of Bald Head Island newsletter, 1982.

The lack of golfers during those early days might be explained by James Poole. "You didn't go over to BHI to play golf," he says. "You went to work on your house, to socialize, to take in nature on walks, to get away … That was the enjoyment of the island. It wasn't like other beach destinations; this was a whole different game." But precisely because the fairways were so often vacant, it allowed the avid golfers to let loose and be themselves.

Take Billy Dunlap, for example. Billy claims not to be a nudist, but given a few of his experiences on the island, it might not always seem that way to an outside observer. In the '80s, there still weren't many houses on the island, and often nobody else was there aside from his buddies and a single security guard (who happened to be his brother-in-law). It was during those times that he'd claim that if you wanted to, you could play golf naked on Bald Head Island.

One day, while teeing off with two of his friends, he decided to prove that theory. When Billy got to the second tee, a thought crossed his mind: *Here is an opportunity to do something that I may never be able to do again in my life.* Since there were no houses on the second hole at the time, he turned to his friends and said, "I'm going to play this hole naked."

At first they laughed, but Billy wasn't joking. As they carried their bags off the course, Billy went back to the second hole wearing nothing but his boat shoes. He lined up at the tee, cracked his club against the ball, and ended up making a par.

According to some, that's where the story ends. They say Billy made the hole, threw his trunks back on (everyone wore t-shirts and swim trunks on the course back then), and returned home. But according to others, Billy decided to keep his streak going (in more ways than one) and played the entire eighteen-hole course in the nude.

People have asked him over the years which version of the story is true, but no matter how much they pried, Billy would neither confirm nor deny any details. Now, only Billy Dunlap can tell you for certain. But consider this: if a man plays one hole of golf naked, what on Earth is going to stop him from playing the rest?

Today, the thirty-five-acre Bald Head Island golf course is a sought-after attraction all of its own. The eighteen-hole championship course, redesigned by Tim Cate with sandy areas mixed with native grasses and Miniverde® greens, is known for its beautiful and challenging fairways.[28]

Over the years, traditions cropped up on Bald Head Island. Harper Peterson remembers sitting around with Bynum Tudor, Anne Pickering, and a few others when someone suggested holding a golf cart parade. So they did, with forty carts participating the first

---

[28] "Golf," The Bald Head Island Club, accessed February 10, 2022, bhiclub.net/golf.

Mildred and Bo Caperton in one of the subsequent golf cart parades. Photo courtesy of Sharon Lightbourne.

year. "We didn't think to take pictures, but it was windy and hilarious," he says. "It's a fantastic tradition that's stood the test of time."

Every Easter, Alex Mitchell and his family would get together to paint eggs. His grandmother had ten children, and every year she tried to get as many of them together at the island as she could—sometimes up to forty relatives would join together in painting dozens and dozens of Easter eggs. It was an unforgettable tradition that eventually led to an island-wide event.

Several women of the island would color eggs late into the night; the next morning, the men would create concentric circles around the lighthouse. Then all the adults would hide the eggs within those circles. "If you were under five years old, you would search in this circle, and then it expanded out by age," Harper Peterson explains. "The kids had so much fun with the hunt that it established the yearly egg hunt and helped establish the church, too."

In the 1980s, art became a focus on the island. Patricia Young, an artist who specialized in watercolor and pastel, first held a show with Malcolm Fleming at the *Young One* house. "It was so fun and we almost had a sellout," she says. The Smith Island Art League began when Malcolm and another fellow artist, Nancy Giacci, approached Patricia about presiding over the proposed league, which she accepted. Over the years, the League formalized into the organization it is today.

In addition, "No Boundaries," the international art colony, was started by Kent Mitchell. "The Mitchells donate the artists' accommodations at *Captain Charlie's* 1, 2, and 3 for two weeks in November while they make art," Plunkett Dodge says.

Fishing was another popular endeavor during both the pioneer and outfitter eras. "There's really nothing to compare to Bald Head Island when it comes to fishing," says Charlie Young. Surfcasting, gillnetting, shrimping, flounder-gigging—the islanders did it all. They fished at the Point, from their decks, and along the creek. They invested in equipment, like young Bob Hayes with his $5 Zebco rod and reel, and intervened when friends got stuck hip-deep in the mud flats.

Sometimes the catch was large, sometimes small, and sometimes not what they were expecting. One time Leslie Thomas was elected to pull in the gill net after everyone else went home to shower. Standing in the murky water alone, she worked quickly to finish before the sun went down. But when the net brought her face-to-face with a five-foot shark, she didn't bother to complete the task. "To this day, I rarely go in the water unless I can see what's around my feet," she says.

James Poole recalls how Malcolm Fleming, the well-known artist, and his wife, Carolyn, ran a fishing camp out of the fire station. "We enrolled our son in the camp and he caught his first fish—a big bass—in the lagoon right near our house. Alligators later came in and ate up all the bass, but the fishing camp was really well attended and it was a lot of fun. Later it became the fishing school through the Conservancy."

In 1985, Thad Wester, as the founding president of the Bald Head Island Conservancy, took over the fishing school and added a tailgate-style jambalaya cookout as a fundraiser. Hence, the camp soon came to be known as the Thad Wester Fishing School. Its purpose was to educate adults and children about the importance of conservation and preservation while teaching them how to effectively fish the waters of Bald Head Island. The first day of the school consisted of classroom instruction followed by an opportunity to practice casting reels and throwing nets. Then, after fishing on the final day, the participants and instructors gathered for a traditional fish fry featuring the freshly caught fish.

Cookouts, bonfires, and fish fries—no matter what you choose to call them—weren't just relegated to the fishing school. On any given evening, a call could be put out over the CB for a TPP—"Total Population Party"—at the Point.

As families from around the island arrived, they'd circle their vehicles on the sand. Children would dash into the ocean for one last late-afternoon swim as the teens gathered driftwood and kindled the fire. Peanuts, beer, and cocktails were shared by adults as they prepared the food. Sometimes entertainment was provided; Bill Poole is reported to have sung "The Lord's Prayer" on at least one occasion, and Pat Thomas frequently played his accordion and guitar. And then finally, after eating their fill of fish or shrimp or whatever was on hand, they sat under the stars in front of a crackling fire exchanging stories until the rising tide forced them home.

Long after the kids grew up and the next era of residents arrived on Bald Head Island, these original couples continued to put out the call. As Pat Miller says, "One of my favorite traditions is when a group of us old-time Bald Head Islanders get together and take glasses of wine to the beach to watch God as he paints a sunset for us."

Unidentified person (left), Bo Caperton (middle), and Bynum Tudor (right) during a "Total Population Party" at the Point. Courtesy of Sharon Lightbourne.

Not all dinners took place at the beach, of course. Plenty of entertaining occurred year-round in the homes everyone had worked so hard to build.

Charlotte Dunlap fondly remembers hosting dinners at their house, especially Thanksgivings.

Lee Wester hosted omelet parties. "Everyone was given a plastic baggie with raw scrambled [whisked] eggs inside," her daughter Ginny explains, "and each guest would then add their choice of condiments such as cheese, onions, peppers, tomatoes, bacon, ham, and so forth. The bags would then be dropped into boiling water until the eggs were cooked."

At Christmas, Lee and Thad Wester invited any residents on the island who didn't have family with them to join them for a potluck lunch. Lee would provide the turkey and stuffing while others brought all the sides.

Then, of course, there were frequent Generator Society cocktail parties and, much later, the annual Generator Society Gathering. For nearly twenty years, these devoted

Back row, left to right: Ken Cosgrove, Bill and Billie Jean Berne, Unknown, Harriet Poole, Sara Ward, Joe and Buris Crowell, Kitty and Earl Congdon, Joanna and Bynum Tudor. Front Row: Pat and Charlie Young, Pat Thomas, Thad Wester, Eleanor Cosgrove, Lee Wester, Elva and Harry Schmulling, Frank Poole. Date unknown.]

pioneers returned to Bald Head Island in order to reunite and celebrate their friendships and beach house adventures.

It's important to note that an invitation to any social function in the early days, regardless of location, carried with it the unspoken request to bring your own ice. "It's something most people take for granted today," Bill Dunlap says, "but back then, ice was an invaluable luxury." This crystal-clear frozen commodity was treasured so much that it came to be called "Bald Head Diamonds."

"In the island's scorching summer months, ice was worth its weight in gold," Billy explains. "While there was an ice maker by the creek access that the residents could use, it wasn't always working."

"Two of the most important products in those early days were ice and gas," Gene Douglas agrees, with emphasis. Indeed, according to Pat Thomas, when it was known that guests were coming, they were "beseeched to bring along as much ice as they could manage."

Although many islanders owned small refrigerators with freezers, they were only able to freeze one or two trays of ice at a time—hardly enough for a houseful of people for a single day, let alone a full week. This eventually led several members of the Generator Society to pool their money together to buy a community ice maker.

This worked well … except for the time an undisclosed islander used all the ice to make peach ice cream without fair warning. "Not only was the ice cream not shared, but the rest of us were without ice for the rest of the day," Thad Wester recalls. Fortunately, it was an isolated incident.

These are just a few of the Generator Society members' memories. As Harriet Poole concludes, "How fortunate we were!"

Chapter 50
Surviving the Storms

Whenever a hurricane was on the horizon, many vacationers returned to their mainland homes. But back in the 1980s, some of the islanders who chose to stay would head to Old Baldy. The lighthouse had weathered countless storms for more than a century, so everyone figured if it had been there that long, it wasn't going anywhere. So, people hauled food, water, and grills up to the tower, where they held parties to ride out the hurricanes. This tradition lasted years and years before the deteriorating Old Baldy was eventually locked up for everyone's safety.

Sometimes there were reluctant partygoers, such as when Polly Fish's dog had just given birth to thirteen puppies, or when the Bunns missed the last ferry. Unwilling to stay in their homes, they rode out the hurricane in the lighthouse, along with a white owl. "When we'd poke our heads up above the concrete wall, the powerful winds literally took our breath away," Buck recalls.

Every hurricane delivers an aftermath, which often involves heavy flooding. Beth Kapil likened her backyard to Lake Michigan. "It was the most amazing thing to see the island under three feet of standing water," she says. "There was one high spot on the golf course behind my house, like an island of its own. And you talk about wildlife! It was an experience unto itself. The birds—the ibis, the herons—were all looking for a dry spot in our backyard and it was wonderful to see. We had plenty of food and we made everything on the grill. I hate to say I enjoyed it, but I'm not sure I would do it again."

Merry Bradley remembers the day she and other volunteers were canoeing through chest-high water at the villas when they saw a familiar face wading toward them. It was Joe Lee with his parrot perched on his shoulder, walking through the flood like it was nothing—when most people wouldn't have dared walk through those waters for anything. When Merry asked what he was doing, he replied matter-of-factly, "We want to check on the house."

Plunkett Dodge recalls evacuating to Southport during Hurricane Diana. When she and her children returned, they had no water for a long time. "I did the laundry in the puddles in the dunes," she laughs. "It was wild, but it was also really fun, especially with two young kids; a sense of freedom like nothing else."

Hurricane-force winds often caused additional damage. Oz Osborne and his wife, Robbie, for example, purchased a villa in '88 along the eighteenth fairway. "It had a large glass window in the living room," Oz says. "After one storm came through and blew the window in, Robbie flew down to get it replaced and purchased a new living room suite. The next thing we know, another storm came through and did the same thing. She had to fly down and get yet another living room suite before I ever saw the first replacement."

The Eure family experienced even more costly wind damage. Given that their house was situated on the beach, Thad Eure was concerned about it being washed out to sea. So, before the storm landed, he hired a trucking company to dump several tons of sand in front of his house. Unfortunately, his attempts to mitigate damage had the opposite result. During the storm, strong winds blew open the front doors, causing all the sand to blow straight into the house. When James Poole went to check on them, Thad handed him a shovel. "There was at least a foot or two of sand in his living room," James recalls.

Not all weather events on Bald Head Island have been hurricanes, of course. There was the time, for example, that a waterspout came ashore directly over the Congdon's home. Kitty Congdon recalls being pulled down to the floor by a house guest seconds before the *C Turtle* seemed to come alive. "The house shook like a rattle for what seemed an eternity," Kitty explains, "and when it stopped, the front wall of the living room had been pushed in ten inches." Looking out at their deck, she saw that all the patio furniture had been either blown into the lagoon or onto the seventeenth fairway. Yet even more surprisingly, Earl had slept through it all.

Meanwhile, Frank Poole, Gene Douglas, Thad Wester, and Bill Berne had been enjoying a round of golf when the sudden rainstorm forced them to flee for shelter to the pro shop, where they watched the waterspout rise over the *C Turtle* and head toward the golf course. It is reported that they later finished their game, but regardless, Millie Caperton recalls that "all those who had been out on the golf course were soaked to the skin, and they all came to the *Milbo Hilton* to use my clothes dryer."

Of course, there have been plenty of regular thunderstorms over the years as well. Harriet Poole recalls the time a lightning strike caused about $600 in damage to their stereo, TV, and the coveted ice maker. Thankfully, it didn't catch the house on fire, and no one was injured.

As scary as storms can be while in the relative safety of a home, they can be downright terrifying at night … in a boat … especially when they're least expected.

In 1975 at Thanksgiving, Marty Marshall and her parents, Bob and Gladys Marshall, came to visit Bald Head Island to talk about the house they were planning. When they arrived at the creek-side dock, Marty's brother had to use the bathroom and accidentally left the light on in the information house.

They hadn't expected to spend that night on the island, but when the Westers invited them to a party, they knew they would need their luggage. So, Marty went with her dad and a few others to retrieve their things from their car on the mainland. Their first leg of the journey went off without a hitch. But as they headed back to the island near dark, a storm began to brew.

Unable to outrun it, they got caught in high, swelling waves and torrential rain that struck the boat like machine-gun fire. With no navigational equipment aboard, they had no idea where they were headed as the boat rocked around in the darkness. Their biggest fear was that the ship would be swept out to sea—which could prove fatal since there were no life vests. Tired, cold, and worried, they strained their eyes in the darkness. Eventually they glimpsed a dim light and used it to guide them back to shore, where they discovered the source of their rescue: the bathroom light Marty's brother had accidentally left on earlier that day. Within an hour, they were all safe, clean, and dry at the Westers' party—the storm outside nothing but a memory.

Chapter 51
That's Just the Way It Was

"If there was a word for the people who built up BHI, it would be 'caring,'" James Poole says. "I would have to say that was the hallmark of that initial group. It was the culture that started on the island and just continued and continued as it got bigger and bigger. It was a natural family atmosphere along with the joy of the island and what it represented."

"Camaraderie" is another term that applies to the Generator Society. In fact, it's a word that four different Generator Society members themselves use to describe the relationship they have with each other:

Bill Berne—"There developed a camaraderie—a closeness—among those early settlers. We would always check when we got to the island to see who was there to plan a get-together—inviting them for cocktails or planning a cookout."

Bippie Grubbs—"Very soon a tremendous camaraderie existed and a closeness that is usually achieved only after many years of friendship."

Charlotte Dunlap—"Bonding, togetherness, concern for others, camaraderie, sense of helping all members of 'community,' group activities like fishing at the Point, etc."

Eleanor Cosgrove—"All of those families got along so well and everybody helped each other out because we didn't have a hardware store, you didn't have anything there. So everybody had these huge tool rooms. They would borrow from one another and it built community and camaraderie."

"Camaraderie" is a term that denotes respect, a willingness to serve, and, as James Poole describes, humbleness.

"That was the beauty of it," he reflects. "No one knew how much money anyone had. And if you could tell that they had money, they were almost immediately ostracized. Even though Bald Head Island was started by people with means (most of the Generator Society members' professions were in the service world, such as doctors, restaurant owners, etc.), there was no show. They were all so unpretentious about who they were, but there were some big names over there in the '70s."

Christi Golder remembers the popular island advice: "You have to leave your Mercedes on the mainland." Golf carts were the great equalizers of the island; everyone drove around in the same thing. "We're marketing to Docs in Birkenstocks," was a common phrase at her office, referring to residents like Dr. Wester and Dr. Berne and Dr. Poole. Respectable folk and never too flashy, since Bald Head Island wasn't meant to be a country club scene.

Christi wanted people to understand that the island wasn't some uptight community where you'd worry about what you were wearing or how your hair was styled. "There are no 'good hair' days on Bald Head Island, anyway!" she laughs. "It's not a pretentious place—never has been—and, God willing, it never will be. It's just a place where you can relax."

Pat Miller agrees. "The pioneers of the island were drawn here because of their love of living in harmony with nature. We loved that nobody cared who anybody was or what their title was."

Such mutual affection was contagious, even spilling over into the relationship between the Generator Society members and John Messick, the point of contact of the developer in the 1980s.

"John Messick was always very accommodating," Bippie Grubbs remembers, "and somehow he was always there when you needed him." This included the time Mr. Messick, after discovering Reddy Grubb's forgotten wallet, fired up the McKee Craft boat and caught up with the ferry mid-river in order to return it to Reddy.

In addition to being accommodating, John was also skilled at placating. As Bynum Tudor explains, "'Sixty to ninety days' was something John Messick always said when anyone asked when anything would happen on BHI. Power? Running water? Ferry system? All of the questions apparently ended with the same answer: sixty to ninety days. It became a running joke because most everything took ten years to finally happen."

Yet despite frustrations, challenges, difficulties, and the occasional disagreements, everyone was willing to help anyone in need.

Whether it was agreeing to stash steaks in their refrigerator when a neighbor's fridge broke, or allowing a friend to connect to their water pump for two weeks, or pulling stuck vehicles out of the sand, or putting out a garage fire, the early residents of Bald Head Island were willing to help each other however they could.

And oftentimes that meant, if you were a doctor, that you didn't get a break from your job. Many medical emergencies happened over the years at Bald Head Island, but one in particular has gained notoriety among Generator Society members.

It involves the time Charlotte Dunlap was hanging clothes out to dry and stepped on a concealed piece of taught fishing line that acted like a trip wire, causing an attached fishing hook to propel into the calf of her right leg. "It was very large and rusty," Charlotte recalls.

Knowing she needed medical assistance, she tracked down Thad Wester, a physician, who was working on the airstrip with Pat Thomas. When they saw her leg, they took her to Pat's home and sent Charlotte's sister-in-law to gather medical supplies from Thad's house.

Bald Head Island's first—and presumable only—surgery took place on the picnic table in Pat's screened porch. "It was quite a scene," Charlotte recalls. "The surgeon (Thad) was drinking a beer as was the scrub nurse (my friend Inez), the patient, and a number of other spectators. Pat sat nearby playing 'Rock of Ages' on his accordion."

The operation was quickly completed and declared a success. Indeed, Charlotte fully recovered within a week.

James Poole and his father, Frank Poole—both pediatricians—would also often receive calls over the CB asking them to come treat a sick child. "We'd take care of everybody there," James says. "I remember one weekend I saw like fifteen different kids that were sick with one thing or another. I told my dad, 'This is not a vacation. And you know, I'm medically liable for all these people I've treated and they're not even my patients. Bald Head needs to treat these people.'"

His concerns were valid. One time shortly thereafter, when neither of the Poole doctors was on the island, a child came down with a severe illness that required evacuation to Wilmington. "He was lucky to live," James says.

That was when James developed the "first responder" program on Bald Head Island. "We had no emergency plan at first, so I worked out a plan of action with Southport's emergency room." It also prompted the Mitchells to establish an EMS presence on the island at all times.

When summarizing their experiences during those early years on Bald Head Island, the pioneers and outfitters exude appreciation.

According to Bill Berne, "We endured hardships of varying degrees, but with the passage of time these all pale in comparison to those special times we shared during those days." Billy Dunlap states that life on Bald Head Island made you see the world from a different perspective and consider things you never had to before. "It was challenging for sure," he says, "but it was also a lot of fun."

"The troubles with the generator and the dependence on the tides were simply a part of island life then," Irma Caroon explains. "That's just the way it was. A small price to pay for the beauty and solitude of those early days."

James Poole agrees, having relished "the closeness of family, the closeness of God, being attuned to nature, and cherishing the land."

For Eleanor Cosgrove, the island is always going to be home. "We still have such a heart for BHI," she explains. "It's like the sea turtles; we always go back."

Brock Rozich agrees. "Though the island is vastly different today than it was in years past, that feeling of being home still remains. Old Baldy is guarded now, no longer free to explore whenever you want. Gone are Eb and Flo's, the River Pilot restaurant, the inn, and the Ice Cream Shoppe in the harbor. Pirate Pizza has been replaced, and Indigo Plantation no longer sees the traffic of the *Revenge*, *Adventure*, and *Sans Souci*. The boat house has finally succumbed to the elements, though its footprint remains. But in their place, new locations serve as the foundation of memories for the younger generation enjoying Bald Head today."

"And most importantly," Brock continues, "the shoals still remain free to explore, unspoiled by the development we see on other barrier islands. The forest preserve still welcomes explorers to see the 100-year-old trees nestled along its routes. The lending library still provides a good read for the rainy days on the island. And Captain Charlie's—small, cozy, and intertwined with nature—still keeps watch, serving as a reminder of the relationship between humans and nature that the keepers of this island have worked so hard to protect. But I would be lying if I said that after a long day on East Beach, I don't miss the low-pressure cold shower, and a cold, fifty-cent can of soda from the gazebo."

"It was a part of history you'll never get again," Dena Cosgrove concludes.

Captain Charlie's Station. Photo courtesy of Pat and Charlie Young.

---

[29] According to the Bald Head Island Ferry website, the *Revenge* was named after Blackbeard's flag ship *Queen Anne's Revenge*, and the *Adventure* was named after his supply ship. "Adventure," Bald Head Island Transport, accessed February 10, 2022, https://baldheadislandferry.com/adventure.

[30] *The Sans Souci,* which means "without worry" or "carefree" in French, refers not only to the relaxed BHI lifestyle but also to an eighteenth-century rice plantation along the lower Cape Fear River that shared the same name. "Sans Souci," Bald Head Island Transport, accessed February 10, 2022, https://baldheadislandferry.com/sanssouci.

Acknowledgments

I thank my husband for always rooting for me with whatever I take on. Thank you to the Schenck School in Atlanta and my mom's dedication to my education. Billie Jean Berne, Pat Miller, Ginny Wester, and Patricia Young: Thank you for your guidance, your time, and the encouragement along the way.

To the more than forty islanders and Generator Society family members who allowed me to interview them—thank you. Without your willingness to share your experiences and/or documentation, this book would not have been possible. I am truly grateful.

I want to give a *huge* shout out to Dalene Bickel for making this book come to life; I couldn't have done it without you (learn about her writing and editing services at www.lasting-legacies.net). Thank you to Rachael Huerta Carpenter of National Geographic for the cartography skills to see my map dreams come true.

Unless otherwise noted in the text, all the stories and historical data used in this book were obtained from my first-person interviews with islanders, Generator Society surveys conducted by Bill Berne (used with permission from his wife, Billie Jean Berne), and the Old Baldy Foundation's online archives and subject files made publicly available at (https://drive.google.com/drive/folders/1uEV1UbBDZx10HNDH4wxY3CsRsih8Y-vfG).

—Mary-Kathryn Moore

About the Author

Mary-Kathryn Moore calls Asheville, North Carolina, her home base but spent 2020 and 2021 working remotely in Mexico, Canada, Bald Head Island, and Honduras, where she and her supportive husband showed their daughter how to take in the beauty of nature in different environments. She's an avid birder, candy connoisseur, and graduate of the University of Georgia with a career in the business world.

www.ingramcontent.com/pod-product-compliance
Lightning Source LLC
Chambersburg PA
CBHW062035290426
44109CB00026B/2635